LIFE AND I

An Autobiography of Humanity

BY

GAMALIEL BRADFORD

GREENWOOD PRESS, PUBLISHERS
NEW YORK 1968

TO

AMBROSE WHITE VERNON

WHO WILL UNDERSTAND

"Les Autres forment l'homme: je le récite."

MONTAIGNE

CONTENTS

LIFE AND I

.·.

CHAPTER I
LOVE AND I

I

THIS is the book of I, not of one particular I, but of the general human I that fills and makes the world. The first personal pronoun, which in English is unfortunately a single capital letter, applies not only to me, but to you, to him, to her, to untold millions of human beings, present and past, and it is on this general basis that I have ventured to use the subtitle: 'An Autobiography of Humanity.'

The universal community of the I is the justification for constantly introducing my own feelings and experience. Without such justification, to do this would be worse than impertinent, it would be uninteresting. But my experience is so largely your experience, and your experience mine, that it is possible to shift easily and naturally from one to the other, and to use both to illustrate each other in different phases and different connections.

I

LIFE AND I

Emerson, in the great First Series of Essays, remarks, perhaps somewhat metaphysically: 'There is one mind common to all individual men: every man is an inlet to the same, and to all of the same.'[1] A writer far different from Emerson and far more widely read, Mark Twain, puts the same thing more practically, urging that every year he lives, he becomes more convinced that he and other men are alike and that what virtues he has are the virtues of others, while the vices of others are all to be found in him. Of course this does not mean an assertion of complete identity, which would be patently absurd. The truth simply is that, while all have the same fundamental traits and impulses, these develop in different cases in different forms and degrees. It is the fundamental resemblance that makes it possible to enter into others' lives, and gives the study of them profound and inexhaustible interest. It is the endless superficial difference that gives that study all its variety and piquancy. Voltaire, who had probably known about as much of the varying surface of human nature as it is given to any one man to know, said that, with a little imagination and one's own heart, one might understand everything in humanity. And Sainte-Beuve, whose experience was equally vast, declared that one can get to the very depths of human life, without ever going out of one's self.

In one sense the I is the greatest thing in the world. There have even been those who maintained that it was the only thing in the world. It may also be said to be the littlest, pettiest thing in the world. It has its times of being overweeningly conscious of its own greatness. It is pitifully, tragically aware of its own pettiness, also, of its isolation, its remoteness, its utter incapacity of getting away from itself. From the time the I becomes conscious at all, from the time it exists, it struggles passionately to assert itself, to enlarge itself, to stretch out, reach out, and draw into itself more and more of the surrounding, entrancing, perplexing world. As it makes this effort to enlarge, to enrich, it becomes more and more conscious of the involving, netting, strangling limits, until, in extreme cases, its life is a life of rebellion, of desperate endeavor to escape, to go free, to shake off the trammels altogether, and even, if necessary, to overcome, to subdue, to destroy the I itself, if it cannot be extended to that largeness, that completeness, that universality, which alone would seem to satisfy its desires.

The subject, the theme, of this book is not

metaphysical. It makes no pretence to philosophical theorizing. Neither is it didactic or theological or inspired by any impulse to make the world over or to make it better, or to make men other than they are. In the words of Montaigne, which I have chosen for my epigraph: 'Others form men; I recite them.' My endeavor is simply to make a dramatic presentation of the greatest dramatic struggle of the world, that between the I and the Not-I, between this everlastingly aggressive, all-engrossing self and the objects that attract or repel it, the manifold, conflicting forces against which it must assert itself triumphantly, or else tragically and miserably perish.

To achieve this presentation I mean to deal in the earlier chapters with the most marked phases in which the I asserts itself, 'Love and I,' 'Power and I,' 'Beauty and I,' 'Thought and I'; then in a central chapter, 'Christ and I,' to typify the greatest agency which has ever been developed for overcoming the I; and in the concluding chapters, 'Christ and Not-I,' 'Christ and More Than I,' 'Christ and I and God,' to show how this and similar agencies have been applied.

II

In beginning it is necessary to look a little more closely and analytically into what I mean by the I. Here again I do not wish to be abstrusely metaphysical, being quite incapable of anything of the sort. But where the I is to play such a central part, it is necessary to give some clear, simple indication of the sense in which it is used.

I begin, then, with the universe of real and imagined sensations and feelings, beyond which we have no knowledge, no conception of anything. There is at any one time only a small group of conscious sensations, amplified always by the vast regions of the sub-conscious, which may be called into direct consciousness, or may come thither without calling. In this conscious universe the sensations and feelings are grouped by what we call relations, such as the fundamental one of identity and difference, which constitutes the first element of existence, and further, time, space, causality, with their various complications. The term I may of course be applied to this universal whole, but in that case it is so inclusive as to mean little.

In this vast complex of the universe the philosophers have sought untiringly to establish a distinct, consistent metaphysical ego, but their efforts are

5

too conflicting to be very satisfactory. Sometimes they take it for granted that the I is perceived by direct intuition. Sometimes they get their results by processes of reasoning which astonish more often than they convince, as in Royce's endeavors to build up the I on the complicated structure of the time relations. One of the most recent and most interesting of such efforts is that of Professor McDougall, in the last chapter of his 'Abnormal Psychology,' an effort based partly on the complications of dual and multiple personality, though it may seem to some that the solution is more difficult even than the problem. The amazing variety of all these theories hitherto somewhat impairs their conclusiveness, and I myself am disposed to accept the bare universe of sensations and feelings with their varying relations, without introducing any metaphysical ego into it whatever. This disposition is much confirmed by comments like that of Professor Overstreet, in his paper on the application of relativity to the individual, read at the Philosophical Congress in Cambridge, Massachusetts, in 1926: 'The individual is and is not himself; is and is not changing; is and is not other individuals.' ²

In the general maze of sensations and feelings

one particular group of real sensations is, however, so significant, so predominant, that the designation I seems most of all and naturally to belong to it. I mean the group of sensations constituting the body or physical organization. It is a curious thing that the processes that go on within this physical organization are almost entirely hidden from us, we can arrive at them only by indirect and very unreliable deduction. Yet the external body is the most inescapable object in our universe. Wherever we go, whatever we do, the body is always with us, always forces itself upon our attention, and no matter what other metaphysical content may be given to the I, it must remain primarily associated with the body at all times and everywhere.

In two most important respects this I-physical organization of ours differs from every other object in the universe. First, a whole group of real sensations is localized within it and nowhere else, and these sensations are among the most grossly and substantially important of our lives. Elementary sensations, like smell, taste, and touch, including the physical phenomena of sex, exist in the body only. The complicated sensations which we include under the name pain are wholly in the body, and nothing in the world makes the I more sharply, exclusively conscious of itself. That vaguer realm of sensation known as feeling belongs also strictly to the body, love, hate, anger, aspiration, and many others, above all fear, the correlative of pain, which in its many manifestations haunts the I as inseparably and perversely as its shadow.

To appreciate the significance of the body as localizing all these intense sensations, it is interesting to let one's imagination run over the universe with the suggested possibility of all sorts of sensations of which we know nothing whatever. Suppose the taste sensations were localized in the leaves of trees, so that, every time the wind ruffled them, we were aware of delicate thrills such as are associated with delicious food or drink. Suppose the sex sensations were in the same manner associated with some external object, or objects. Suppose that, if the bark were torn from a tree, we should feel actual pain, or if a stone were struck or shattered, we should get the agony that comes from the tearing or shattering of our own nerves. Suppose, further, as one easily may, the existence of sensations different in kind from those that we enjoy or suffer, a bewildering multiplicity of ecstasy or torture of which, with our present organization, we have no knowledge at all. All this brings clearly home to us the sharp existence, the peculiar identity of the I-body in itself, with nothing in the universe to parallel it or to equal it in importance.

The second extraordinary difference between the body I and all the rest of the world lies in the direct obedience of the body to the will, to desire accompanied by effort. In the whole vast universe, as we know it, there is not the minutest object outside of the body which can be directly affected by our wills except through the intervention of bodily agency (barring of course such hypnotic and magnetic action as is yet but very imperfectly understood and often hypothetical). Even within the body the action of the will is distinctly limited. Certain muscles are under its conscious control. We can lift the hand or foot, or govern the wonderfully complex machinery of the organs of speech. We cannot add a cubit to our stature. We cannot obliterate a mole or a hair on the surface of the body by any amount of willing. But in the external universe nothing is directly subject to our wills, absolutely nothing. Whether we seek to remove mountains, or to dislodge the smallest pebble from our path, it can be accomplished only by the agency of the body and by the will acting through that agency.

The physical I is then primarily distinguished by these vastly important peculiarities. From the earliest period of life we are accustomed to give it a name to be known by, and this name becomes almost as essential an element of the I as the body itself. Also, when time comes into the account, we have the past history of the I accumulated in consciousness under the name of memory, and this again becomes a most essential element in the I complex. There is no such thing as memory except in connection with the body, so far as we definitely know, and all our knowledge of the past comes to us directly or indirectly through memory, and so is part of the history of the bodily I.

It is possible, also, to carry on an analysis of character in connection with our own I, character being simply a complex of verbal qualities, and those qualities being again simply generalizations of the habits of thought and action (including speech) of the physical organization. But this process of analysis is so delicate, so elaborate, so complicated, that we are more apt to apply it when forced to gain a knowledge of others than in dealing with ourselves.

For it is evident that the world swarms with other physical organizations, apparently similar to this overwhelmingly predominant one that constitutes the I for us. These other I's, if we call them so, are mere phenomena, mere pictures, mere groups of external sensations in the external world, and to direct consciousness they can never come to be anything else. As to the sensations and feelings that exist within them we can know nothing, nothing whatever, except as we infer them on a basis of what goes on within ourselves. These other I's are as remote from us as the pictures on a wall, or the stars in heaven, so far as getting ourselves into any real communication with them goes. Yet we move among them in the closest daily intimate contact, and it is essential to our own activity, to our own comfort, to our own existence, that we should have some knowledge of them and should be able to predict their action to some extent and to discern the possible bearing of it on our own. Therefore we are perpetually, more or less unconsciously, forming in regard to them the generalizations of speech or action to which I have referred above, and which we call qualities of character. These generalizations are as vague, as fleeting, as uncertain as the winds of heaven. Yet,

such as they are, they form our only means of
divining the nature of the other I's about us, and a
close and careful investigation of them is the first
requisite to the conduct of our lives.

As I am not prepared to assert the complete
identity of the I with the body, so I will not assert
that all the experiences and instincts of the I are
associated with bodily self-preservation and propagation. Nevertheless, there are thinkers who do
assert this, and at least it may be said that these
instincts are directly or indirectly so prominent in
our conscious life that a discussion of the I must
encounter them at every turn. The element of
propagation will form the central subject of this
chapter; that of self-preservation, in its varied
manifestations and conflicts, will be dealt with in
the chapters that follow.

III

Besides the overmastering instinct to preserve,
maintain, and develop the bodily I, we have, then,
the instinct to reproduce it, in Lucretius's phrase,
to pass on the torch of life in manifold and ever-
varying forms from generation to generation. In
the most elementary kinds of living creatures this
process of reproduction may be monosexual, but

in all the more complicated organisms it is accomplished by the embodiment of life in two sexes, which combine in different fashions to reproduce their like, of one sex or the other. The more elaborate reproductive instinct manifests itself, however, primarily in the mere blind enjoyment of the sexual act, which, in order that the object may be accomplished, becomes, brief as it is, the most fiercely pleasurable of all the sensations known to living beings. When the reproductive act has resulted in conception, and so fatally in birth, the parents, especially the female, are further impelled in the highest degree to nourish, to watch over, to develop their offspring.

Yet it is curious to note how at all times the intense assertion of the primary, personal I is bound up with all these reproductive manifestations. The care of children involves toil, it involves forethought, it involves infinite patience, it involves sacrifice, even at times the sacrifice of life. Yet we know how fully the parent finds, or hopes to find, his or her account in the growth and future of the child. The father looks forward to the child's triumph or achievement as his achievement. How would it have been possible without his effort, or imaginable without the inheritance received from him? The mother sees herself pointed out as the teacher of the man who is to teach others, to do strange, great things, to benefit the world unspeakably. Above all, children represent unfulfilled ambitions and desires. The man who grew up with wide hopes and aspirations, who felt that he had in him to build a great fortune or a great reputation, but failed owing to the miserable intrusion of casual circumstance, believes that his son will do what he could not, sees in his daughter's career, in the concert-hall or in the movies, what he ought to have achieved but was accidentally prevented from achieving.

And always parents look to their children for comfort and support — spiritual, if not material, for response, for sympathy, for understanding, and how rarely do they find it! For the child too has its own colossal I, which, from infancy, begins to assert itself, to clutch the world for itself, to disregard everything in the mad necessity of accomplishing its destiny of living. In too many cases the attitude toward the parent is one of respectful indifference, at most of obvious and conscientious duty merely. The material is attended to and complied with, or too often it is not, but the spiritual connection is not thought of, because on

the child's part there is no need of it. He has his
own playmates, his own companions, his own fellows, like in age, like in habits, like in training, who
understand him. Why should he concern himself
about the wishes and longings of the antique past?

Perhaps the separation and failure are even more
pathetic where there is real devotion, real desire
to understand, on both sides. Somehow there is
always the barrier, the insurmountable barrier,
which forever sets your I apart from mine in all
cases, which seems especially difficult to pass where
there is difference of age, and which erects itself
most stiffly when there is physical nearness and
daily contact. In the empty, thoughtful, infinitely
suggestive night you discover a thousand things
that you want to utter to those dear to you. There
are secrets and longings and mysteries which you
think they can share and ought to share, you yearn
perhaps to talk to them about God, the greatest
secret and the greatest mystery of all. Then you
meet in the crass morning light, you exchange
trivial gossip, tawdry matter of the day, foolish
and futile jests, and the greater, deeper, more passionate questions die upon your lips. It seems a
sheer impossibility to utter them.

There are times when children concentrate all

the joy and hope of life; yet there have been few more devoted fathers than Thomas Moore and Charles Darwin, and Moore said, 'My anxiety about these children almost embitters all my enjoyment of them,' [3] and Darwin's expression is much the same: 'Children are one's greatest happiness, but often and often a still greater misery.' [4]

IV

But the procreation of children is a comparatively minor conscious element in that which, as a clever English novelist puts it, 'Non-conformist ministers and reviewers call sex, and ordinary people love.' [5] Self-preservation may be at the bottom of eating and drinking, but we think very little of it, when dainty banquets are set before us. So the thought of nature's purposes in reproduction enters precious little into the charm and the mystery and the magic of loving. It is a glamour diffused over the whole wide world. It enthralls both sexes alike, or not alike, but equally, the woman with the subtle, unescapable, all-engrossing habit of withdrawing seduction, the man with the bolder, more vehement activity of pursuit and capture. There is the infinite exploration, and satisfaction, and tireless renewal of curiosity, there

is the halo of dream and romance which spreads
its glow over the hard, glaring, remorseless surface
of arid, daily fact. No age is entirely exempt.
Scarcely out of infancy the boy and girl playing together touch hands and lips with a secret conquer-
ing thrill that they do not comprehend. The flame
bursts out and rages through middle life. In age
decorum quells the manifestation of it, but it lurks
ready as ever to disorder the world on the slightest
excuse. Love is never better pleased than when it
can play tricks with dignity, can overturn solemn
procedures, can bring gravity upon its knees and
make it descend to the fantastic follies which en-
chanted and bewitched its youth. The aged and respectable high-priest Calchas, in 'La Belle Hélène,'
murmurs, 'If I had followed my true vocation, I
should have been a man of love and pleasure.'[6] So
do we all, all murmur in our hearts; for the grave,
staid business of the world only diverts us when it is
impossible, or we think it is impossible, for us to be
loving any more.

The splendor and the glory of love, which are
obscured by the crowding insignificance of daily
life, get their revenge fully in imaginative literature, and the poets and the dramatists and the
story-tellers fill the world with varied incarnations

of the fundamental impulse of the earthly Venus. Again and again aged critics and serious thinkers protest against this. Love, they say, is after all a minor matter, and the manifold other efforts and struggles of men are far more important. Why not make literature of these? And the poets and story-tellers endeavor to do so, but the rare exceptions only serve to prove the rule, and still, still the en-croaching, engrossing matter of love contrives to find its way.

Sometimes it is love in its more artificial, super-ficial phases. As we have the vast unrolment of the Spanish drama, hundreds of plays all turning upon the same clever and unreal intrigues, the same gambols of puppets twisting and turning up and down in the hands of the cunning, laughing Master. Or again, as in the modern realistic novel, we have the crude, ugly, violent, physical aspects, developed in deforming, distorting, repulsive de-tail, but still and always with the same mighty, elementary instinct at the bottom.

We have the comedy of love, its inexhaustible, romantic charm. We have it centuries ago, in all its pastoral grace, in the idyls of Theocritus: 'Thus let me sit and sing, having thee in my arms, love in my arms, and beneath us our flocks feeding, and the blue, divine Sicilian sea.' [7] Or in the most exquisite of prose idyls, 'Daphnis and Chloë,' which gives at once the primitive permanent formula of love meeting all sorts of difficulties and obstacles till all the obstacles are overcome and the lovers are united in undying bliss. And the formula has run unchanged for two thousand years, as Miss Austen summed it up: The art of 'keeping lovers apart in five volumes.' [8]

And we have the tragedy of love, love thwarted, broken, tortured, by untoward circumstance or by itself, from the time of Helen and Phædra through Shakespeare and Racine down to Dumas and Ibsen and the latest drama of the present day. And it is hard to tell which charms or enthralls us most, to see love triumphant and rewarded, or to see it asserting the destructive glory of its passionate sway in the midst of jealousy, cruelty, despair, and overwhelming fate.

But the distilled essence of love in literature is certainly the love-song, as we hear it echoing through the ages in all its varied witchery of passion and grace. Curiously enough at the very beginning we have the delirious outcry of a woman, which has been heard so rarely until recent years, and the Odes of Sappho reach at once the acme of the lyrical expression of love. And there is love subtilized, analyzed, intellectualized, tormented into a thousand remote forms, as in the mediæval singers, or in Petrarch. And there is love simple, direct, intense, breaking away from literary consciousness in its ardent fury, as we find it in Catullus long ago, and in Heine almost within living memory, and perhaps in its most delicate clarity of perfection in the Elizabethan lyric, at any rate in Shakespeare, who struck the immortal note:

> What is love? 'Tis not hereafter.
> Present mirth hath present laughter,
> What's to come is still unsure.
> In delay there lies no plenty.
> Then come kiss me, Sweet and Twenty,
> Youth's a stuff will not endure.

It is surely love that makes the fascination of all social gatherings of the mingled sexes, gatherings so tedious to the preoccupied man of the world, but so full of magic for those who are still under the charm. Take the whole story of women's dress, and love is written in it everywhere. All the curious arts, all the little, subtle developments and changes, all deal with love and are meant to suggest it. At once to hide nakedness and to reveal it, this is the whole secret of dressing for women, and it is curious and sometimes pathetic to see the purest and most innocent cultivating this secret to the full, without being in the least aware of it. Take the dress of to-day. When women began to wish to live like men, they aimed to dress like them, yet the outcome of this was simply to develop and distort every element of man's dress that could suggest and enhance the feminine obsession of sex.

Take dancing. The ardor of exercise, the charm of rhythmic movement no doubt enter into it. But who questions that Venus is hidden beneath? The permitted proximity, the look, the touch, the quick, glowing whispers, all make love and dancing synonymous from the start and sufficiently excuse those who protest against it from the standpoint of Puritan rigidity.

And over this social tumult of loving is the light, dainty, always solvent grace of laughter. Quick wit, swift, fertile exchange of airy nothings, allay the too direct, intense fervor of amorous excitement, allay it and at the same time intensify it. All over the wide dance-hall you will note the quiver of laughter and catch the gleam of smiling merriment. Or again, in the amusement park or the public garden, in hot summer evenings, you will hear shrieks of laughter cutting the dense shadows, then perhaps an hysterical giggle, and then — silence under the unbabbling stars, which have seen so vastly much of love and never told it.

For, as Sterne says, there is no passion so serious as lust. And under all the laughter and all the brilliant, complex fabric of social convention and manner, there are just the plain physical facts, which the social fabric is created to conceal. 'Madam,' said Heine, to the prudish lady, 'I suppose we are all naked under our clothes.' So we are all naked, and if you like, naked brutes, under the elaborate garb with which the slowly contrived convention of centuries surrounds us. 'L'amour,' said Chamfort, 'est l'échange de deux fantasies et le contacte de deux épidermes.' [9] The exchange of the fantasies is vastly complicated, and subtle, and difficult. The other ——

If we are seeking documents on the other, we may read Havelock Ellis's 'Psychology of Sex' (I never have), or most of us may feel that nature supplies us with quite documents enough. The overwhelming domination comes upon men directly from childhood. It comes upon women perhaps not quite so directly, but even more absorbingly and persistently. It riots through the growing vigor and breadth of life with ever-renewed and self-renewing variety

and splendor and often horror. And who will say
for a moment that it is wholly absent or overcome,
even in withered age? If grave and solemn men,
idolized statesmen, skilled physicians, reverend
divines, and incontestably virtuous matrons would
or could ever give us a genuine, deliberate, complete
record of their sexual lives, what revelations there
would be to disturb a complacent world! And I
often think of the remark of Sophocles in Plato,
of that Sophocles, whom, as Arnold says,

Business could not make dull nor passion wild,[10]

when he was asked, 'How does love suit with age?'
'Peace,' he replied.... 'I feel as if I had escaped
from a mad and furious master.' [11] So often we
think we have escaped when we have not!

It is obvious that if this mad, engrossing impulse were allowed to run riot, it would upset the
world. Hence the curious fabric of conventional
hypocrisy, propriety, decorum, with which civilized
social life has come to protect itself, and by which
we never speak of what we all think. This decorum
varies oddly in different periods, as, in the height of
the Victorian age, ladies were never permitted to
have legs and never went to bed, but retired. We
think we have got happily rid of all that, yet how
far even now is our language from our thoughts.

The license of literature is one way in which we endeavor to make up for the restrictions of polite social intercourse, yet even literature, so long as it pretends to be literature and not simple pornography, in its frankest moments practises a more or less delicate reticence in comparison with the facts.

I amuse myself sometimes by imagining a sexless world, one in which the present methods of reproduction should be eliminated and something substituted that should be of a purely mechanical nature. What an extraordinary revolution would ensue! Life would be swept clear of many of its refinements, its mysteries — and also of so much of its charm.

We do not live in a sexless world, and the more or less necessary checks, restraints, and, to use the modern slang, inhibitions, distort the sex instinct from its normal, healthy, animal course, into a thousand abnormalities and morbid symptoms. The ingenious Dr. Freud has made a psychology and almost a philosophy out of these abnormalities, detecting the sexual impulse in our most ordinary activities and even, or most especially, in our dreams. It has always seemed to me that Dr. Freud's zeal somewhat outran his discretion, and I am glad to find so sane an authority as Professor

McDougall, while recognizing Freud's undeniable ability and achievement, disputing the extreme of his sex explanations and hinting that Freud himself is now inclined to reduce them, even the cherished Œdipus complex.

The abnormalities are insistent enough, however, no matter how you explain them. There are the more physiological abnormalities, such as perversion, Sadism, Masochism, words become so pleasingly familiar to the astonishing youth of the present day that one has no hesitation in using them anywhere. In fact, they appear to be taught in the kindergarten, with, or without, the alphabet. The delicate analysis of Landor has long, long since been disregarded: 'From the mysteries of religion the veil is seldom to be drawn, from the mysteries of love never. For this offence the gods take away from us our freshness of heart and our susceptibility of pure delight.' [12]

More familiar and more interesting to most of us are the less physiological features, though perhaps they are quite as abnormal at bottom. There are the strange, overmastering obsessions, which make love, at its height, appear nothing less than sheer insanity, the doubts, the questionings, the abject submissions, the unreasoning jealousies, the strange

intermixture of ecstasy and torture. Love tears at
its own heart, tears at the hearts of all about it,
dissects, torments, in the futile effort to accomplish
the impossible. 'We wish to be all the happiness,
or, if that cannot be, then all the unhappiness of
what we love,' says La Bruyère.[13] These extravagances affect not only the unbalanced, the consti-
tutionally morbid and diseased. Minds otherwise
so supremely powerful as those of Lincoln or Keats
are temporarily unhinged, thrown hopelessly into
disorder, by the attack of amorous insanity. And
not only the great, but you and I and the most
prosaic, healthy man in the street are subject to
being at any time utterly deranged in the same
manner.

The whole discussion is complicated by the fact
that the sexual impulses do not stand by themselves
in complete isolation, but are at all times more or
less bound up with other instincts of a different
order. Dr. Freud's method is to emphasize the intrusion of sex interest into every phase of existence.
It seems to me far juster to stress the presence of
the deeper and more enduring elements of self-
preservation in the midst of sex, and I am interested
to find a recent high authority asserting this in regard to the much-cherished Sadism and Maso-

chism: 'The facts which are held to justify this assumption [of a purely sexual basis] are largely facts of which the true explanation is to be found in the working of two independent instincts that are well founded in comparative psychology, namely, the instincts of self-assertion and submission.' [14] There is the instinct of power, which appears in acquiring such complete mastery over another. There is the sense of dependence, by which our weakness seeks for external, artificial, alas, too often purely imaginary strength to comfort and support it. And everywhere interwoven with the purple tissue of love there is the thread of vanity, the suggestion of conquest, so vastly complicated with the coquetries of women and the infidelity of men. As again, there is the desire for intellectual sympathy and comprehension, which is a basis of friendship and love both.

But, whatever the theories, whatever the explanations, there is no doubt about the mighty, unhinging violence of love in almost all our lives. Sexual disorder has been the furious enemy of some of those who best understood it and analyzed it most deeply, as for example, Sainte-Beuve, whose novel, 'Volupté,' is one of the most curious dissections of love in its spiritually morbid forms. It has been the ruin of men who studied it and depicted it with unfailing curiosity and skill, like Maupassant and Jules Lemaître. Not only in its irregular and more licentious manifestations does it work damage. How many a genius has been undermined and sapped and destroyed by the steady pressure of marital relations, sometimes physiological, sometimes psychological. Even in what appear to be the more wholesome aspects the danger is always there, and we have the remark of Thomas Moore, who knew: 'More mean things have been done in this world under the shelter of "wife and children" than under any other pretext that worldly-mindedness can resort to.' [15]

Yet who can resist the charm? And no doubt the danger and the ruin make it greater. Who has summed up its passionate absorption better than Catullus?

> Odi et amo. Quare id faciam, fortasse requiris.
> Nescio, sed fieri sentio et excrucior.[16]

Compared with that torturing, devouring ecstasy, the rest of life seems dull and null and tame and void, so that one is almost tempted to say that apart from it there is no life, and to envy those fortunate lovers, the Romeos and Juliets, who, in one fashion or another, have gone out in the height and rapture of it, thus forestalling and escaping the slow decay of time, the hideous invasion of decrepitude, and the ugly revelations of plain daylight existence which that enthralling moonlit glamour quite obscures and utterly dissolves away.

V

In all the complication of perplexities involved in the tangled skein of love there is none more perplexing than the varied phenomena of choice. Even in the animal world the process of selection for mating is not always easy to understand. But when it comes to the human animal the developments are so baffling that to explain them after the fact is hugely difficult, and he who would undertake to predict them beforehand would be a prophet indeed.

Sometimes the choice comes all at once, overwhelmingly, and love at first sight, if not unusual, is by no means so unknown as some suppose. Again, the process is so gradual, that the victims, as in the novels of Miss Austen, do not become aware of it until it has taken place. Goethe founded his elaborate and rather tedious 'Elective Affinities' on the theory that there were spiritual affinities, of something the same nature as chemical, which made souls restless and unstable until they could find repose in the combination that naturally belonged to them; but the theory is difficult to understand and still more difficult to apply. Sometimes the selection seems to rest upon contrast. The grave seeks the gay, the weak the strong, the silent a quick and lively tongue, and *vice versa*. Or again, like seems to be drawn to like, and similar qualities are accentuated and perpetuated by proximity and association. Especially is the play of choice astonishing in its utterly irrelevant flights and vagaries. A woman who is distinctly plain, who to most men, if not unattractive, is utterly indifferent, will find in the end some man who adores her. A man who has scorned all the eminently suitable matches chosen by his friends, will finally pick out some worthless creature, some one whom he ought perfectly to understand and does, knowing at the same time that she can never understand him; yet he will bestow upon her unlimited worship pathetically worthy of a better object. And there is the chief tragedy of all, when love pours itself out with complete self-abnegation and meets no return, sometimes from mere waywardness and coquetry, sometimes when there is the best will in the world but no possibility of an answering gleam.

And this tragedy, old as mankind, and capable of being repeated in indefinite forms, has never been put with more compelling simplicity than in Heine's brief sentence: 'Sie war liebenswürdig, und er liebte sie; er aber war nicht liebenswürdig, und sie liebte ihn nicht.' [17]

There are apparently persons with whom love is by nature more or less extensive, and who are ready to bestow it upon any fairly attractive member of the opposite sex who happens to be present, and to transfer it to another with comparative ease. But love in its real power and grandeur is certainly only in the obsession which fixes itself upon one supreme object, making that object, not perhaps forever, but for the time, the one element in the universe that counts:

> I was not, save it were a thought of thee.
> The world was but a spot where thou hadst trod.[18]

This is the love that makes life over, and transforms existence with a golden alchemy beyond any other conceivable. What the supremacy of the one object is, is admirably indicated in George Eliot's phrase: 'To have her enter the room was like placing a significant figure before a row of ciphers.' It is this single obsession which works such disaster as the tragedy of Keats. It is this which carries unlimited delusion and deception with it, by which plain, ordinary flesh and blood take on a divine, enthralling radiance and glory, and mere mortals are for the time transformed into gods and goddesses.

For the time only, alas, in this unenduring world. The radiance fades, the glow disperses, mere common flesh and blood get to be seen as they are, long, long before they become what they finally must be. The hard, prosaic strain of marriage brings more or less of disillusion for every one, no matter how the romantic ardor, which dies so hard in all of us, may resist and rebel. In many cases, in these days of easy divorce, love does not stand the strain at all. In many others the final adjustment is effected, with more or less of labor and difficulty. Then the growth of habit, the development of sweet associations of infinite daily need, develop an enduring affection, which may be essential, may be deeper in its long rooted hold than the original passion, may have its charm — but it is not the madness of love, and never can be.

In this connection, I have found it of extreme interest, in my psychographical studies, to trace the attitude of wives. Women, who in Flaubert's phrase, mistake their senses for their hearts, who

at any rate succeed in making an intricate com-
mingling of the two in a fashion which more humdrum men can never quite achieve, women in marriage fight far more desperately to retain the delusion than men. Hence results the curious mixture
of acute, bare understanding with devoted love,
and the strange fact that it is perfectly possible for
a woman to maintain for the same object an immense devotion and a condescending patronage,
if not even an obscure contempt. In two most
interesting cases, those of Mrs. James G. Blaine
and Mrs. Benjamin Butler, I was able to get the
documents necessary to study this wifely relation,
and no brief phrase can possibly throw more light
upon it than the sentence of Mrs. Blaine: 'I do not
say that he is the best man that ever lived, but
that of the men whom I have thoroughly known he
is the best.' [19] Long, long comment might be made
on that.

Then there are those who passionately refuse to
accept the disillusion, who will not content themselves with the very plain tissue of domestic affection in marriage, but who rove with unabated ardor
in the pursuit of an impossible ideal. Dr. Johnson
said of the case of a man who had been unhappily
married and who married again, in a few months

after his first wife's death, that it was 'the triumph of hope over experience.' Life is the triumph of hope over experience. Love, above all, is the triumph of hope over experience. And some deluded persons rove the world over, seeking to make experience out of hope. With men the quest quickly and infallibly turns into a mere cynical indulgence of the senses. In women the hope is harder to kill, and with specimens like George Sand, in whom the blend of sense and spirit is quite inextricable, it flourishes indomitably, madly, till age kills the senses altogether and relegates the amorous ideal to a world that shall be better than this, or at any rate different.

VI

And always, under the play of the senses and the passionate quest of the spirit, there is just one thing, the effort of the I to enlarge or to escape itself. And it seems as if, with only one individual, this might be accomplished. To diffuse one's I in the vast universe, even to scatter it among the fleeting drift of phenomenal I's all about us, may well appear impossible, chimerical. But when two I's, alone in the void, strive madly to blend their identities together, it almost seems as if they must succeed.

LOVE AND I

There is the delusion of mutual understanding, one of the most seductive and intoxicating of the lures of love. Because one has so much to impart, one assumes that to the beloved one can easily and finally impart it. In the throng and multitude of those who can never comprehend, there seems to be just that one select spirit who is attuned to ours, and to whom all our hopes and struggles and despairs may be made known. He or she, and he or she only, can understand us: we are sure of it. There is the delusion of physical contact. We urge, we press, to force the hungry spirit through the avenues of the body, to meet the other spirit that leans towards it with an equal hunger. The old Roman poet Lucretius has depicted with unequaled fierce power this mad struggle of bodies to be melted, dissolved, lost in each other, in the desperate effort to blend souls.

Then the inefficacy of the physical contact becomes too glaringly apparent, and after the most ardent intensity of it, the two souls are left further apart than they were before. And the delusion of understanding fails. You pour out your whole inner life, or you endeavor to pour it out, since even in the effort you feel the sheer impossibility. But you have no evidence whatever that it is understood, and so often you have lamentable, pitiable evidence to the contrary. Again, you try to grasp the inner life of the beloved, and still, still it slips away and eludes your search. Under the beautiful forehead, and the penetrating eyes, and the clinging lips and their murmur, you feel that there is hidden a universe of secrets, and do what you will, you can never, never enter into them. And those who have the most to give and make the most endeavor to give it, most feel the depth of failure in desolation and despair.

The poem of Matthew Arnold, which I have quoted elsewhere, in connection with the passionate effort and the subtle analysis of Sarah Butler, best sums up how vast the failure is. We are all like islands, says Arnold, set off forever in an immense, impassable ocean: we strive to reach the other islands, and we cannot.

> But when the moon their hollows lights,
>   And they are swept by balms of spring,
> And in their glens on starry nights
>   The nightingales divinely sing,
>
>   . . . .
>
> Oh, then a longing like despair
>   Is to their farthest caverns sent,
> For surely once, they feel, we were
>   Parts of a single continent.
>
>   . . . .

LOVE AND I

A god, a god their severance ruled,
And bade betwixt their shores to be
The unplumbed, salt, estranging sea.[20]

And so the I, during all its existence, in this world at any rate, is left tragically, incurably, brutally alone.

CHAPTER II
POWER AND I
I

LOVE in the narrower sense is the passionate effort of the I to come into contact with one other. But even before this desire has manifested itself, and long after it has faded, there is the broader, if less intense, disposition to connect oneself with many human beings, in fact with humanity at large, in the manifold different relations of social life. In its more elementary forms this tendency is evident enough in the gregarious instincts of animals and it is highly and curiously developed in the social insects. At the very bottom of the tendency there is the obvious impulse of self-preservation to secure protection in weakness by combining many units together. Weakness is most oppressive, most overwhelming in solitude. And the company of others, even when no stronger than ourselves, does something to remove the sense of exposure to infinity in utter isolation. Also, for all purposes of accomplishment, there is a manifest gain in being associated, as is so wonderfully shown in the activity of the bees, or the ants, or the beavers.

POWER AND I

As the I asserts itself in seeking protection, so it asserts itself, a trifle more subtly, in giving it. Nothing affords us the sense of power so much as having others look to us and depend upon us. This appears not only in all sorts of complicated forms of human relation, but in our connection with the domestic animals. They protect us, they assist us, but there is also a splendid feeling of power in our mastery and control of them, as in easy and skilful horsemanship, and all these relations express themselves in a reciprocal affection which is akin to the human in its intensity and which some persons find more satisfying.

More subtly still, the I shows itself in the social relation in the desire to excel, to surpass others in an endless variety of ways. Nothing more strengthens our exceedingly frail confidence in ourselves than the knowledge that we are able to outdo others in something. This knowledge may build itself up — dangerously — in sheer self-elation in solitude; but it is most richly and naturally developed by constant contact and comparison with other human beings.

Still more elaborate as a social motive, we have the impulse to mingle with our fellows, in order to know and understand them. Mere, simple curiosity has endless play here. The vast and supple intelligence which has developed for the ends of self-preservation, does not find in this enough to occupy it, and if it is turned wholly inward, preys destructively upon itself. But it has an inexhaustible field in the study of other human beings, both in their likeness and in their difference. And this study is not merely curious, but is absolutely essential. We must know others, and judge their conduct and their characters, in order to frame and shape our own lives. Therefore the observation of men and women becomes at once one of the most fascinating and one of the most profitable of pursuits, and all of us carry it on, in some shape or other, some with clearly conscious analytical effort, and others with instinctive, but often none the less acute, practical watchfulness.

In this mutual study the most effective, and certainly by far the most interesting agent, is conversation, the exchange of thoughts and feelings, or what pass for such, by means of those rich and extraordinarily varied, though also extraordinarily imperfect instruments, words. There are persons, and some very wise ones, who seem to find conversation one of the most satisfying, as it is certainly one of the most curious of the minor arts that make up the great art of life. As to the best methods of practising this art of conversation there will always be difference of views. Probably the best of all is to think nothing about it. I used to hold that the triumph of conversation was to draw out your interlocutor, to make him feel that you were interested in his interests and to lead him to talk about them. Experience has modified this view, though it is doubtful whether it can ever modify fifty years of practice. People do not always like to be drawn out, especially when they think it over afterwards, neither do they always wish to discuss their own affairs, at least too openly. The greatest experts seem to conclude that conversation should not be a monologue, nor a piece of skilful interviewing, but, as far as possible, a fair exchange, in which you should talk about your own affairs and interests sufficiently to give your correspondent a reasonable excuse for talking about his. Yet, after all, the secret of conversational charm is difficult to analyze, and some persons can talk about themselves for hours, while others in doing the same thing get infinitely wearisome in a few minutes.

I confess, however, that, probably for purely personal reasons, I have always found conversation extremely disappointing. No doubt I expect too much, but what I have expected I have never or rarely got, though I have talked — or listened — with some who should have had remarkable conversational powers. And I have been interested to find a lady, who had been everywhere and met the most brilliant men of her day, the Countess of Albany, confirming this impression. Madame d'Albany is speaking of the delight of books: 'They are the only pleasure of a reasonable person who has passed a certain age; for conversation is mediocre, and ramblingly inadequate, and always uninformed.' [1]

Our social interest is, of course, never indiscriminate. All men and women may interest us, but all do not interest us equally, and at any rate we do not find all equally attractive. In other words, something the same play of choice shows itself in friendship as in love, and often with the same inexplicable vagaries. Certain I's we seek with clinging ardor, and others we avoid, with an antagonism approaching repulsion. And here, as with love, there is the same eager desire for spiritual contact, and the affection founded on that desire is one of the great charms of life. Yet, again as with love, there are the hopeless and impassable barriers. Emerson says, 'we descend to meet.' We may go further and say, we descend, but we do not meet. There is the perpetual striving, with the perpetual lack of achievement. We have so vastly much to say, and we cannot say it, and sometimes the pressure of a hand will convey more than the dumb striving of the lips. The nearer the physical proximity, the more difficult the contact. And those who have the gift for it can pour out by letter what freezes on the tongue when those we love best are close beside us. There is even the odd paradox that a skilled writer will give to the perfectly unknown and unfeeling public, secrets that he cannot possibly communicate to those he loves best. As Montaigne has it: 'How curious and amusing it is that I can tell the public many things that I would never mention to a private friend, and when it comes to my most intimate thoughts and experiences, I have to send my nearest friends to the bookseller.' [2]

Of all the social motives, if not the deepest or most intense, probably the most constant is the simple desire to avoid solitude. The I is averse to being left alone with itself, for such seclusion too fatally brings reflection upon failures, errors, and disappointments. It is strange how often we seek any society except our own, and most of us at all times, all of us at some time, are willing to put up with those who bore us, even with those whom we dislike, for the sake of getting away from ourselves. Weakness, power, affection, distraction, these would seem to sum up the social instinct in its entirety; but of them all perhaps distraction is the most prevailing. Yet the distraction may be full of diversity and charm. And I do not know where the varied delight of it, with all the complex elements of social excitement, are better suggested than in Pepys's description of a royal evening: 'We fell to dancing, and continued, only with intermission for a good supper, till two in the morning, the music being Greeting, and another most excellent violin, and theorbo, the best in town. And so with mighty mirth, and pleased with their dancing of jigs afterwards, several of them, and, among others, Betty Turner, who did it mighty prettily . . . and then to a country-dance again, and so broke up with extraordinary pleasure, as being one of the days and nights of my life spent with the greatest content; and that which I can but hope to repeat again a few times in my whole life. This done, we parted, the strangers home, and I did lodge my cousin Pepys and his wife in our blue chamber. My cousin Turner, her sister, and The., in our best chamber; Bab., Betty, and Betty Turner, in our own chamber; and myself and my wife in the maid's bed, which is very good. Our maids in the coachman's bed; the coachman with the boy in his settle-bed, and Tom where he uses to lie. And so I did, to my great content, lodge at once in my house, with the greatest ease, fifteen and eight of them strangers of quality.' [3]

II

Through all these social and human contacts the desire to excel appears in manifold forms. There is the desire to surpass others in birth and breeding, and to show it by manners, or the lack of them. There is the desire to excel in dress, or in appointments or in social ornament of every kind. Since we cannot get away from the I, and are so keenly conscious within ourselves of its pettiness and insignificance, let us at least inflate it with external appearance, as much as we can. And some do this obviously and obtrusively, and some veil it, and in some the working is so indirect that they themselves are not at all aware of it; but with all of us it is there in some measure.

A comparatively petty and trivial, and yet most curious and instructive manifestation of this universal desire to excel, is the habit of sports and games. The distinction between the two I take to be that in a mere sport, as in races, for instance, there may be competition with others, but one's own action is not affected by, is not interrelated with, such competition. In a race the presence of a competitor may add to the excitement, but the race could in itself be run as well against time alone, without any competitor at all. Even in such complicated contests as golf this is substantially the case. In games proper one's own play is constantly modified by the action of one's opponent, and one is incessantly on the watch to observe his mistakes and to profit by them. To be sure, this definition would include boxing and fencing with games; but it is likely that the game instinct is involved in both of them, as distinguished from sport pure and simple.

In any case, the desire to win enters into sports and games both, but more particularly and passionately into games. And there are few things, even of much greater import, in which fundamental character shows out more quickly, or with more amusement or profit to those who are analytically interested in such matters. When money and gambling are involved, the game instinct becomes almost a madness, but even without this incentive, how astonishingly people reveal themselves, how soon tempers are lost, and good manners forgotten. How easily even those who are naturally well bred and good humored will come to insist upon petty advantages, to criticise the errors of partners and gloat over those of opponents! The excitement of a trivial game of cards, which is forgotten in an hour, will make men and women into quite different creatures.

It is hard to say which is more revealing, failure or success. A man who is commonly charitable and kindly, and may be your best friend, will beat you in golf or billiards. He will expand for the whole evening, and will kindly point out to you your mistakes and his achievements, though the slightest reflection would show him that you are quite as well aware of them as he is. Beat him, on the other hand, and his brow is dark, and his lips are closed; or he insists with ardor that he was completely off his game, without the slightest consideration as to where this leaves you and your success. To be beaten at chess or backgammon will put an edge on the most Christian spirit, and I have known devoted wives who had to abandon such games altogether, for the sake of domestic peace.

But the most interesting feature of all in connection with this matter of games comes when the public takes a hand in it. It is something to triumph over your wife or your best friend, in your own quiet living room, and the I will get pure rose-color from it for a day. But to win in baseball, or football, or a prize-fight, before shouting thousands, with millions behind them through the newspapers or the radio, this is perhaps the most intoxicating form of glory that has yet been developed by man. And the wonder of its intensity is equalled by the wonder of its brevity. A baseball player knocks home runs all over the United States, and for ten years his name and his face are known to every man, woman, and child in the country. The universality of his fame is beyond that of Homer or Shakespeare. In another ten years he is gone utterly, or pointed out, even in his vigorous middle life, as a curious relic of a vanished past. In another ten years still, his very name is forgotten by all but the searcher in dusty records. A woman swims the English Channel for the first time. She returns to New York, and is escorted by millions who would never assemble for the victor of the Great War. In six months nobody will know whether she is alive, or dead — or care. Rarely in all the world does the I get a more enormous expansion, or a more complete eclipse.

III

Perhaps the most engrossing and universal form of surpassing others is by the possession and acquisition of money. This enters so widely and so deeply into most other forms that it gains and maintains a predominant importance everywhere. The saints and sages quarrel with it and scourge it. To be sure, Dr. Johnson said, 'There are few ways in which a man can be more innocently employed than in getting money.' [4] But in general the saints and sages do not agree with this view. They point out the insidious, corrupting power of money, in social life, in political life, even in religious life. In theory they both condemn it and contemn it thoroughly. But even with the saints and sages theory and practice are not always strictly in accord.

The form of money-worship changes, though the ardor of it remains the same. Thus the last few centuries have altered the material aspect. Gold, at any rate in America, has largely given place to bank notes. The miser of old times hugged his gold. There was an immense and peculiar charm in the sight and the touch of it. Hence there was immediate hoarding of every kind. There is not the same pleasure in hoarding greenbacks, and the miser, as a mere accumulator and gloater in holes and corners, has largely disappeared. But the love of money and the sacrifice of time and strength and character and even pleasure to it have not disappeared, and never will.

There is the perfectly legitimate feeling that money means independence, and independence is in some ways the greatest thing in the world, the fundamental condition of accomplishment; at any rate dependence is the greatest handicap. To be sure, none of us is really independent, but the dependence that comes in money matters is one of the bitterest to endure and one of the most subtle and far-reaching. How galling and how far-reaching, has never been better suggested than in the words of the poet Gray: 'It is a foolish thing that one can't only not live as one pleases, but where and with whom one pleases, without money. Swift somewhere says that money is liberty; and I fear money is friendship too and society, and almost every external blessing. It is a great, though ill-natured, comfort, to see most of those who have it in plenty without pleasure, without liberty, and without friends.' 5

It is true that, as Gray's last sentence indicates, mere financial independence goes but little way for happiness, and in general the word itself shows that the thing is merely negative. But money means vastly more than negative advantages. It means power. It is this deeper implication that accounts for the eager pursuit of money in a democratic society like ours, where money supremacy has to take the place of aristocratic rank. Europeans are apt to call us money-worshippers, idolaters of the dollar. In a sense we are, but it is rarely for mere financial accumulation. The American business man cares little for money in itself, cares little for the actual pleasure it can bring to him personally. He has no time for such pleasure, no training for it, and any way it could never consume a tithe of what he wishes to gather together. He likes to spend because of the position it gives him. He likes to have his wife and daughters spend. Above all, he likes to give, broadly, judiciously, magnificently. Nothing in the world yields him the sense of power that giving does, or so swiftly brings men bowing and cringing to his feet. He knows perfectly the emptiness of such adulation, but he appreciates and enjoys it, as we all do. The emptiness and the power both are admirably conveyed in an interesting study of the late Frank Munsey. According to this account of him, Munsey admitted that he got no real satisfaction out of his forty millions, and affirmed that to him life was merely dust and ashes. Yet he said: 'I like to have plenty of money about me; I like the feeling of it; I like to strip off a thousand-dollar bill and hand it to some one, or order my agent to buy a piece of property or a magazine or newspaper.' [6] So long as this feeling retains its enormous hold, so long will money continue to be the force in the world that it has always been.

IV

Even more than in these indirect ways, however, the I loves to assert its immediate power over men. This can be done, first, also more or less indirectly, not by actual control, but by influence. There is the influence of example, so vastly greater than any of us appreciate. Some use this deliberately, either with a malicious sense of conquest in steering men downward, or with a high aspiration in guiding them on an upward course. But the influence of example comes far more, collectively, in the lives of all of us, in the slighter habits that are formed by daily association, habits of manner, habits of labor, habits of effort and conscience and achievement. We do not stop to think how immense an influence we exert in this way, but probably there are few greater agencies in the world, for good or for evil.

Then there is the more conscious leading of others, by spoken words, by persuasion, argument. There is the direct, simple influence of one individual on another individual. And here we come into contact with that mysterious instrumentality, speech, so subtle, so evasive, so intangible, so astonishingly effective, yet so difficult to manage or control. It is hard to say whether one is more overcome when one thinks of what words will do, or of what they will not do. They will touch hearts, they will make over lives, they will lead men to heaven or to hell; yet when we try to convey our deepest feelings with them, we stammer and halt and too often have to give over in complete despair.

Words can perhaps do most as between man and man. But their power, if weakened, is also vastly manifolded, when they are poured out by a skilled tongue to masses of men, and here again the secrets of power are almost beyond analysis. What is it that sweeps great multitudes collectively to action which their better individual judgment often condemns? Why is it that the best and profoundest intelligence and the noblest purpose are sometimes stutteringly unable to convey their inspiration, while a comparatively empty head or heart can make a crowd of listeners do what it will? And all these problems of speech power are immensely amplified to-day, and are going to be more so, by the wireless distribution, which makes the influence of the human tongue a thousand times greater than it has ever been before.

And there are printed words, also, agents of power almost beyond estimate. There have always been the great authors, and in the last hundred years there have been the journalists, who make our language, and mould our habits, and think our thoughts for us, and from behind their screen of anonymity exercise an influence all the greater because it is undiscerned and perfectly irresponsible.

This indirect power through influence, can of course be used either for good or for evil. The manifold uses of it for good will occupy us in a later chapter. But we all know how it can be used for evil also, how there are spirits who work continually upon individuals or numbers, to achieve their own selfish purposes, and even in some cases for the pure mischief of it and the malign sense of power that comes from feeling that you can hurt the world, even if you cannot mend it. This influence is nowhere better incarnated than in Shakespeare's Iago, who is indeed always putting forward practical motives for his conduct, but who is so evidently animated by the relentless assertion of the I in the ability to make others suffer.

V

Absorbing and delightful as the indirect exercise of power is, probably the direct exercise of it in actual executive management and control is even more so. Some people are born with a natural aptitude for this; what is more, they enjoy it, make decisions affecting others, take the lead, take responsibility, and find in these things their greatest pleasure and satisfaction. 'I love passionately to be master,' said Voltaire.[7] So do many others. And again still others shrink from mastery as from the plague, and take no shadow of responsibility that they can escape. To such the burden of arranging their own lives is more than sufficient. How any one can possibly desire to arrange the lives of others is quite incomprehensible. To these persons — and I am one of them — it seems sometimes that the ideal of life would be to have to make no practical decisions at all, but to turn over one's conduct in complete obedience to the better will and judgment of others, cultivating not only the wise subordination

55

which is understood by none so well as those born to command, but an abject submission, so that all responsibility might be removed and got rid of.

In connection with these activities of practical management I have always found one of the most curious analytical studies that of success. Why is it that some men succeed, and other men fail? Mere effort will not account for it. The most devoted industry, the most unfailing patience, often leave their possessor a mere hopeless drudge, toiling forever at a humble daily task, with no future and no hope of advancement. Intelligence will not do it. Indeed, it sometimes seems as if intelligence hampered, as if the large and just consideration of various possible courses of action interfered with the quick adopting of any course, which is so indispensable for achievement. Pleasant manners, kindly and sympathetic treatment of others, do not always bring success, though they go far. Even self-confidence, which goes farther, and perhaps farthest, will not, by itself bring a foremost place in the world. And there is luck to be taken into account, the fortunate combination of circumstances, which sometimes seems to go farther than any gift. Take such a case as that of Robert E. Lee. Lee is generally regarded as one of the great military geniuses of the world. Yet, if the Civil War had not come when it did, Lee would probably have lived and died an utterly insignificant colonel of artillery. It takes some of all these elements in combination to produce the result. Yet, even allowing for them all, the problem of practical success remains one of the most curious and puzzling in the world.

It is interesting, also, to consider not only what gives men power, but the qualities that enable them to maintain it. There are some who rule by direct command, by the natural impression of authority. Something dominating in their natures imposes upon others, and makes even the unruly yield to their controlling sway. But in general command is better supported by varying tact and comprehension. The secret of governing men is first of all to understand them. If you can understand them and love them also, you probably go farthest, but the understanding is essential. 'Ah, if I could know the weak point of every one!' said the clever French woman.[8] It does no harm to know the strong points also. As to the loving, Goethe indicated its value, when he said: 'He who feels no love must learn to flatter. Else he will accomplish nothing.'[9] Flattery is a poor substitute, but at least, to make men do your bidding, you must conciliate, you must compromise, you must adapt yourself, never yielding the essential, but learning carefully to distinguish the essential from what is not so. Note how one of the greatest of rulers, Cromwell, handles this distinction. To one lieutenant he writes: 'I advised you formerly to bear with men of different minds from yourself: if you had done it when I advised you to it, I think you would not have had so many stumbling-blocks in your way.' [10] Yet elsewhere he indicates the qualification that is always necessary: 'The Lord give you abundance of wisdom and faith and patience. Take heed also of your natural inclination to compliance.' [11] One must learn to watch, to listen, to read men's souls quickly but thoroughly, in short one must appreciate Lord Chesterfield's praise of attention,[12] which is not only the secret of good manners, and of memory, as he asserts, but of the far deeper comprehension and consequent management of men.

Yet there is something in the born leader's power which is more than authority, more even than insight. There is the magnetism, the force of infectious inspiration, which seems to double men's energy and halve their fears. A great general, a great ruler, will not only make men do what he wants, he will make them want to do it, feel that their highest aim and their highest joy in life is to carry out his designs and accomplish his purposes, and their supreme reward is in his approval. He who can fill his followers with this spirit is the one who goes farthest and gains most. When a certain Southern general was objecting violently to some course of action, he was told that General Lee approved of it. 'Oh,' said he, 'that alters the case. Whatever General Lee says is all right, I don't care what it is.' [13] The leader who can inspire confidence like this will do all that human power can do.

Another interesting element of successful command is the gift of leaving details to others. There are persons who can conceive an excellent plan, who are willing and able to work hard at it, but who fail because they are unwilling or unable to rely upon others for the execution. It was said of even so great a born governor as Richelieu that he 'had in the highest degree the weakness of not being able to disregard details.' [14] It is not perhaps so important to disregard them, as first to choose subordinates who are perfectly capable of attending to them, and then to leave them entirely in the subordinates' care. And this course has the further not inconsiderable advantage that if the plan works well, the original framer can take all the credit, and if it fails, he can shift upon the subordinates all the blame.

VI

Probably the most intensely absorbing and glorifying form of power in action is the military. Man is, after all, a fighting animal, and all the efforts of the Pacifists will hardly make him different. Action of any kind achieves the two great objects of asserting the I and forgetting it, of intense existence and complete oblivion, more fully than anything else. Given bodily health and vigor, the mere exercise of the muscles in all their rich and varied energy is a delight. The use of them for a profitable, fruitful purpose is no doubt the most satisfying afterwards. But the overpowering excitement of personal combat, its varied demand for all the resources of mind and body alike, is probably the most complete means of putting forward our identity and of obliterating it that the world can supply. And when to this intense intoxication of conflict you add the motive of glory, or the motive of honor, or the even fiercer motives of flaming anger and cold persistent hate, you get the most terrible agent of destruction and ruin known to humanity.

A curious phase of the delight in action is the delight in the imagined action of the story of adventure. Doubtless a part of this enjoyment lies in mystery and suspense. But a very important part lies in our imaginary identification of ourselves with the hero and his energetic, furious personal struggles and final triumph. And the pleasure we take is greatly enhanced by the element of contrast. By temperament we may be timid enough, as indisposed as possible to adventurous, courageous action in our own humdrum lives. But we sit in our warm rooms, in our cozy arm-chairs, and revel in the thrill of enduring arctic cold and tropic heat with the hero's mighty endeavor to overcome time and space and the hostility of man. And another curious feature of these stories is their necessary timeliness. They may deal with the far past in subject, but their tone and treatment must be that of the present hour, if they are to move us. Two hundred and fifty years ago Madame de Sévigné was enraptured with the huge romances of La Calprenède, as you and I are with Oppenheim or Fletcher. 'The book holds me like glue,' she says. 'The beauty of the sentiments, the violence of the passions, the great scale of the incidents, and the miraculous success of the hero's redoubtable sword — it sweeps me away as if I were a girl again.' [15] Yet you and I could not possibly keep awake over 'Grand Cyrus,' and even the romantic stories of fifty years ago leave us yawning and unable to penetrate the first chapters.

The delight in action, so absorbing in its most personal aspect, becomes more varied, if not more intense, when it takes the form of command over the action of others with or without participation in it. Here again there is first the element of immediate excitement, which makes all the other pursuits and interests of the world seem tame. When you are used to great battles, balls and sports are dull enough, and Napoleon remarks with a sigh, as to public functions, 'They are the most tedious part of my business: I was not made for pleasure.' [16] Surely there cannot be any completer rapture, or more entire oblivion, than to lead a cavalry charge: it makes you for the moment forget sins and losses and failures and despairs and absolutely obliterates them. This is what General Lee meant, when he said, in the midst of the carnage of Fredericksburg: 'It is well that this is so terrible, or else we might grow too fond of it.' [17] And the fierce, terse brevity of the following description from one of Cromwell's letters, shows admirably what the intoxication is: 'Whilst the enemy was following our flying troops,

I charged him on the rear with my three troops; drove him down the hill, brake him all to pieces; forced Lieutenant-General Cavendish into a bog who fought in this reserve; one officer cut him on the head; and as he lay, my Captain, Lieutenant Berry thrust him into the short ribs, of which he died about two hours after in Gainsborough.' [18]

Back of the immediate action, and the command and control of it, is the exertion of intellectual power, the planning of battles, the planning of campaigns, the handling of vast masses, arranging detail, or having it arranged, distributing and concentrating, so that all the complicated forces involved will work with mightily accumulating energy to one foreseen, predestined end. Of all the examples and models of this military intellectual energy that we know of, Napoleon is the supreme, in his concentrated power, his ever alert and lightning-like activity and direction of activity. I hardly know a finer piece of analysis than his account of the labor of intellectual preparation that went on in his spirit: 'There is no man more pusillanimous than I am when I am making a military plan; I exaggerate to myself all the dangers, all the evils possible under the circumstances: I am in an agonizing state of agitation, which does not prevent my appearing perfectly serene to those about me. I am like a young woman in travail. Then, when my resolution is once formed the whole agitation is forgotten.' [19]

As the stimulus, the excitement of military command, is indescribably alluring, so is the ambition to obtain it perhaps the most acute and keen, if not the most far-reaching in the world. Dumas puts it vividly, in his witty fashion: 'In any army, from the private soldier, to the second in command, everybody desires the death of somebody.' The fever of ambition, of aspiration, of advancement, of promotion, is universal, all-invading. It is in every way proportioned to the splendor of success, and the depression and despair of failure are as deep as the aspiration is high. Here again we have a bit of Napoleon's searching analysis, showing how ambition so becomes a part of the blood and bone that it is hardly recognized as such: 'In fact, I have no ambition . . . or, if I have, it is so natural to me, it is so inborn, . . . that it is like the blood that runs in my veins, like the air I breathe. It never drives me faster or otherwise than the other impulses that are native in me. . . . I have never had to fight for it, or with it: it is never more impatient than I; it moves hand in hand with circumstances and the general current of my ideas.' [20]

And consequent upon the ambition and the success, when it is achieved, comes the devotion, the idolatry, of thousands of followers, to whom the commander is more than a merely triumphant leader, he is almost a god. Incident after incident in the career of Napoleon shows the mad worship of the men whom he had led over and over through imminent destruction and disaster to immortal triumph. But I do not know any one passage which better illustrates such worship than the account of the reception of McClellan by his soldiers of the Army of the Potomac: 'As each organization passed the general, the men became apparently forgetful of everything but their love for him. They cheered and cheered again, until they became so hoarse they could cheer no longer. It seemed as if an intermission had been declared in order that a reception might be tendered to the general-in-chief. A great crowd continually surrounded him, and the most extravagant demonstrations were indulged in. Hundreds even hugged the horse's legs and caressed his head and mane.... It was like a scene in a play, with the roar of guns for an accompaniment.' [21]

It is hard to imagine a more magnificent assertion of the I in power than this. Yet a few months later McClellan was laid aside, and almost forgotten, which recalls the comment of an equally idolized commander, King Henry IV of France, on a cheering crowd: 'It is just the people — if my greatest enemy was standing where I am, and the crowd saw him, they would do as much as they are doing for me, or would shout even louder than they do.' [22]

VII

The fundamental characteristics of the assertion of the I in political power are much the same in many aspects as with military; but there are also curious phases of difference. For example, military command is rarely inherited, since military gifts are so essential to it. In politics hereditary power and aristocratic rank sometimes go with genius and ability, but in most cases we have the strange paradox of perfectly ordinary human nature artificially elevated far above ordinary human beings by hereditary place. No more striking illustration of this paradox can be afforded than is given us in the picture of kings as drawn by the great analysts and recorders. Take for instance Greville's intimate account of George IV and William IV. Here are two persons of perhaps rather less than average endowment, given not indeed absolute power, but a practically arbitrary control over those with whom they come into contact. And as a result the infirmity and pitiful inadequacy of humanity are only the more emphasized. Take the elaborate study of Louis XIV, rehandled and renewed again and again and again by one of the greatest spiritual painters of the world, Saint-Simon. Once more, we have a man of moderate natural gift and common sense, but still in no marked respect superior to you and me, set upon a pinnacle of circumstance, and with all his daily living transformed by it. The contrast between the sceptre and robes and the plain flesh and blood, as Saint-Simon limns it, is one of the most extraordinary and impressive that history affords. And it is not the kings only, but the aristocrat of all orders and types, with always underneath the consciousness of being altogether different from common men and women. Such an attitude of mind is not very comprehensible in the United States, where the possession of millions differentiates, but the possession of grandfathers does not. All the same, aristocratic consciousness has been an enormous force in the world, and perhaps it cannot be more concisely summed up than in the phrase of one of Saint-Simon's great ladies: 'For my part, I am persuaded that when it comes to a man of such high birth, God will think twice before damning him.' [23]

It is only the very young or the very simple who believe that these elevated stations carry happiness with them. To read the memoirs of the Margravine of Bayreuth is enough to convince any one that sovereigns may be miserable with the depth of human misery. To read Greville and Saint-Simon is enough to make one understand that a king on his throne may be one of the most lonely and isolated creatures upon earth. A wall shuts off such a person perpetually. He cannot know his fellow beings as they are, nor they him. They may obey him, they may flatter him, they rarely love him, and if by any accident they do so, he can never be sure of it. And, as we all know, such arbitrary and unlimited power degenerates into strange corruptions and vices. What it will do to poor human nature has never been better illustrated than in the extravagant follies and depravations of the earlier Roman emperors, of Nero, of Caligula, of Heliogabalus. They were just common creatures like you and me, and the I in us might have been capable of the distorted excesses of power with which it ran riot in them.

Far more interesting than those who are born great, or who have greatness thrust upon them, are those who achieve it. To begin with, there is the motive of passionate, persistent ambition. Some men seem to be born with the overwhelming desire to climb to the top, to command and control others, to get the reins of the world into their hands, and to be seen, known, and remembered as doing these things. The ambition is not always confessed so frankly as with Frederick the Great: 'The satisfaction of seeing my name in the gazettes and afterwards in history seduced me.' [24] But it burns with more or less fury in many young hearts and in not a few older ones. Alexander Hamilton wrote, at the age of twelve: 'Ned, my ambition is prevalent, so that I condemn the groveling condition of a clerk or the like, to which my fortune etc. condemns me, and would willingly risk my life, though not my character, to exalt my station. . . . I mean to preface the way for futurity.' [25] Others have felt the same at a far later period, and have often written it.

Given the ambition, there are the methods of rising. If you live in an aristocracy, you may make war upon it, by appealing to the oppressed people. If you live in the American democracy, you may make your way by a thousand arts and devices, sometimes commendable, sometimes less so. Brains are a help, the intelligence which sees far and thinks deep, though brains by themselves go a surprisingly little way. The gift of organization is an immense help, the faculty of making men work together and all combine their powers to the end you have in view. Tact, persuasive genius, all the score of forms of the social instinct are an immense help. The President of the United States may have brains; he must have good manners and wear a frock coat with grace. But perhaps the greatest gift of all is the gift of words, and this fact most makes the pessimistic despair of democracy, not realizing, when they complain of it, the two cardinal facts, that democracy is still young and has to learn its business, and that the experience of a hundred thousand years has not produced anything better. But words do rule the world of democracy, catch phrases, current slogans, neat and pointed and telling inventions of the tongue. And the amazing thing is that words can go so far as they do, with so little behind them.

So you rise and rise, and there come the supreme moments of triumph, when you seem to have reached the top and can go no further, as in the great crisis of Cromwell's fate in the dissolution of the Long Parliament; 'And I do dissolve this Parliament. And let God be judge between you and me.' [26] And then your power wanes and your hope wanes, or if it does not, you come to feel the emptiness of both power and hope, and the incapacity of either to satisfy that devouring I, which can never be satisfied in this insatiable world.

One of the most curious elements in the study of political power is the constant intertwining of selfishness and unselfishness, of the desire to advance oneself and the desire to benefit others. It is probable that the most completely self-centred despot alleges to himself some larger interest, some more extended identity of his own interest with that of his country and his subjects. There can be no question of a certain sincerity in Napoleon's writing: 'All my moments, my entire life, are employed in fulfilling the duties which my destiny and the people of France have imposed upon me.' [27] Yet who doubts that Napoleon was colossally first to himself? And from his egotism there are all stages to the self-forgetfulness of Washington and Lee, in their patriotic age, when mere earthly glory had become as indifferent as earthly glory ever can be.

A striking and typical instance of this achievement of political greatness is the contemporary career of Mussolini in Italy. One conjectures in the Italian dictator's case an entirely sincere devotion to his country and desire to make it fortunate and prosperous and great. Yet it is easy to see how personal power and the intense assertion of the I can be mingled with these patriotic motives and become more and more engrossing at every step. And in every other case of dictatorship that has ever been known the personal element has encroached until in the dictator himself or his successor absolute power has met with a fall even more sudden and overwhelming than its rise.

The limits, the so to speak negative qualifications, that we have already considered in regard to practical success generally are perhaps most marked in this political connection. A supreme self-confidence is the first requisite of achievement in the political world, and it is doubtful whether self-confidence often goes with a very widely extended knowledge of human life and history at large. Such knowledge breeds humility, not confidence, and humility, while an exquisite virtue, is not a good instrument for fighting one's way in the world. Again, with intelligence. Practical success in politics, as in other things, requires an acute, penetrating intellectual grasp, such as Napoleon had in the highest degree. But broad, analytical general thinking is apt to breed hesitation and uncertainty, to present too many alternatives of possible action, when it is necessary to fix with unerring positiveness upon one course, and that the one instinctively seen to be best. The successful athlete must have a high quality of brain power, but of a very instinctive order, and the intellectual action of the statesman must be of something the same kind.

And as the philosophical intellect does not wholly go with practical success, so one does not look with such success for the humorous attitude. The great statesmen who have had a profound sense of humor, as Lincoln had it in an eminent degree, are rare indeed. There may be plenty of wit, plenty of apt satire. But that subtle appreciation of the comic contrast between the world that is and the world that might be, is extremely damaging to the statesman's progress and advancement. To deal successfully with the world's affairs, you have got to take them seriously, to take men and women seriously, above all, to take yourself seriously. Now to the true spirit of humor, which dissolves the temporal in the eternal, and life in death, nothing is serious, and least of all oneself.

VIII

But it will be said that all this business of statesmen and the rulers of the world is very far away from just plain you and me. We may not be rulers of the world, but the assertion of the I in power enters into little matters of daily life just as much as it enters into the greater doings of generals and kings. Business is a conflict of wills, a conflict of I's, and the greater dominate the lesser, even in the shop and the factory, even in the alley or the mowing field. Everywhere alike we find the I seeking to command nature, seeking to command other I's, and so to assert, to establish, and to affirm itself. This is as true in the home as it is in the street. In every household the same struggle is going on, however the domestic virtues may lenify it. The father, or the mother, or the brother, or the sister, rules, with a gentler or a harsher sway, and the rest submit or depart when they can.

And there is power in the world of women, which might be analyzed endlessly. There are the women who have swayed nations, the Catherine de' Medicis, the Elizabeths, the Maria Theresas, adept at the handling of political power, and combining with masculine methods, the subtler feminine elements of cunning and charm. There are the emancipated women of to-day, with every form of political domination at last brought within their reach. Will they care to use it? For we all know what the sway of women in the world has always been, and their passion for its exercise. The old Cato, two thousand years ago, warned his fellow men that the only way to get on with women was to keep them under, for, he said, if you once let them become equal, they will infallibly end by being superior.[28] The passion of women for social domination among each other is evident enough. And when one considers the power and the influence of mothers and sisters and wives, one is sometimes prone to believe that men have very little to do with ruling the world.

So in small matters as in great, the struggle for power is going on everywhere, and everywhere with the same passion and the same pettiness. In every isolated community, in every country town, there is some one striving for office, and taking every passionate means, of intrigue, of money outlay, of flattery and cajolery and corruption, to obtain it. I myself once held one minor public office, and only one, and to obtain that I manœuvred a worthy man out of it by petty devices and mean insinuations that even now I blush to think of. Yet such things are done in the larger field of politics every day.

And so the fighting I asserts itself all over the

world, tries to make up for the wretched insignificance, of which it is so painfully, pitifully conscious, by maintaining the assured conviction that there are other I's even more insignificant, even more pitiful, over which it can establish an exalting, a comforting, even if only a momentary sway.

CHAPTER III
BEAUTY AND I
I

THERE are few subjects upon which have been
piled a greater luxury of metaphysical definitions than upon beauty, and this has often been
done by persons whose own susceptibility to the
beautiful was not noticeably great. I am not com-
petent to rehearse or criticise these definitions, and
if I were, it would not suit the practical character of
this book. But for my own purpose I adopt an
elementary and very negative distinction, which
has working value. The beautiful, then, is what
attracts us without obvious usefulness, or direct
appeal to the great fundamental instincts of self-
preservation and propagation and to the moral instinct, if separate from these. The beautiful may or
may not be indirectly connected with these great
instincts, but the connection can be established
only by remote and persistent ingenuity.

It is evident that the charm of beauty fails before
the intense urgency of immediate practical need.
We should hardly enjoy a symphony when starving,
or a picture of Titian when suffering with a pain

in the bowels. On the other hand, the magic of beauty, viewed from the standpoint of reception and not of creation, which is an altogether different matter, lies largely in this removal from the immediate, obvious thraldom of the I and its material requirements. When we are weary of ourselves, and seek escape and oblivion, nothing helps us more than beauty in its varied forms. It scatters sordid preoccupations, shakes off trammels and fetters, and sets us free.

It is indeed curious to see the persistent I intruding even in this larger, more independent world, and the merely receptive side of it. There is, for instance, the mania of the collector, who gathers pictures, or statues, or illuminated books, or objects of art of any sort, often with little appreciation of the beauty of the things in themselves, but with intense personal satisfaction in the accumulating and possessing what others have not. And cunning, greed, and meanness will sometimes go to unbelievable lengths in the acquisition of such treasures.

And there is the I of the critic, who studies works of art exhaustively, not so much for pure enjoyment as for the stimulus and excitement of talking and writing about them. Doubtless in most cases, if not in all, the critic would prefer to create, if he could, and in many cases he has tried and failed. Not being able himself to create, he finds it the next best thing to judge and rank and crown or trash the creation of others. Unquestionably this office of the critic has its value, but what chiefly interests us is the unfailing presence of the wayward I in it, perhaps most of all in the criticism that professes to be most impersonal and to impose an abstract standard upon the varied creative genius of the world. And whatever the value of criticism, whatever the usefulness of suggestion and guidance from long study of the beauty of the past, it is the supreme charm of these æsthetic matters that the spirit may move in them without the slavery of too conventional bondage. In conduct we must live, the bravest and the wildest of us, not as we would, but as we should. The conventional standard of morals must be respected to some extent, if we would keep out of jail, even if we are careless of our eminent standing in the community. In the enjoyment of the beautiful at least, we may follow the impulse of our own souls, and if we will, worship what we like, and eschew what we dislike. The trouble is that few of us really will to do anything of the kind.

Yet the charm of this æsthetic deliverance, with no conscious I intruding in it, is incomparable, and those who learn to cultivate it and give it way provide for themselves one of the richest and most enduring satisfactions that this world affords. There is the variety of forms, the ample suggestion of spaces, the delicate grace of curves, the intricate interweaving of lines that blend and fade off with shifting hint of limit and infinity. There is the overwhelming splendor of color, the sharp, voluminous impression of strong contrast, the penetrating, haunting seduction of finer shades, the glory of light, and the subtle, insinuating magic of shadow. And through form and color both there is the intriguing, perplexing relief and intoxication of movement, of change, by which shapes fade and alter, and in their changing take on a swift felicity of grace, which 'teazes us out of thought as doth eternity.' Spirits absolutely lacking in the creative instinct or impulse, spirits of women especially, may derive endless delight from all these things, with neither the ability nor the inclination to express such delight. All that is required is some degree of the sensibility well indicated in the sentence of Eugénie de Guérin, in whom the sensibility was so acute: 'Why are we so framed that a desire consumes us, that a fear breaks us, that a hope possesses us, that a thought may fill us wholly, and that everything that touches us makes us quiver and tremble.' [1]

In some of the problems connected with the plastic arts, painting, sculpture, architecture, it is interesting to note the more or less obvious appearance of the I, in enjoyment, as well as in creation. Thus in the mere skill of imitating it is probable that we always feel the general exaltation of the human I in the particular achievement of the artist. And the same appears in the contrasted gift of selection and composition. The I of different nations manifests itself in different art forms, as in the striking difference between the Greek temple and the Gothic cathedral. So again the I of different ages shows its difference in the varied preferences of artistic production. The most refined connoisseurs of the eighteenth century put Guido and Guercino far above Angelico or Botticelli. The connoisseur of the same order in the twentieth century regards the masterpieces of Bologna as of no account when compared with the primitives of an earlier day.

Of all the arts the theatre is the most popular and the most human, and the charm of the vicarious I in it, as in the adventure stories referred to in the preceding chapter, is the most vivid and the most intense. The drawbacks and difficulties in theatrical enjoyment are obvious enough. As two very different types of artist, the writer and the actor, are obliged to work together, there is always imperfect adjustment and frequently conflict. Furthermore, the theatre involves an extreme complexity of material conditions, both in the presentation and the reception, and thus the pure enjoyment of it is hampered and trammelled to a greater or less extent.

Nevertheless, the fascination of it for all kinds and classes of men has always been extreme, as appears in the vitality with which theatrical production adapts itself to the conditions and requirements of different nations and epochs. There is the fascination of tragedy, of seeing the sins and sufferings and struggles of the I, of others' and therefore of our own, depicted under impersonal conditions which enable us to appreciate its fullest and broadest bearings. Aristotle thought, ages ago, that there was a process of purification by the intensity of pity and terror. At any rate, the absorbed contemplation of human effort in human suffering takes the I out of itself, extends and enlarges it more than almost anything else, and especially when the suf-

fering is ennobled and idealized by the golden light
of imaginative beauty. And then, over against the
tragedy, there is the relieving charm of laughter,
laughter sometimes harsh, cruel, and bitter, sometimes vulgar and trivial, but at its best tender and
human, and even at its worst with a certain quality
of rich distraction which is not to be lightly thrown
away.

So that there are few of us, and those few only
to be pitied, who cannot say with the sweet old
dramatist:

> What an internal joy my heart has felt,
> Sitting at one of these same idle plays![2]

II

The art of the theatre, then, works through two
agencies, acting and words, which do not always
perfectly combine. Literary art works through
words alone, and the typical literary art may perhaps be said to be poetry, since prose, though capable of the most subtle and delicate effects, is too
often used for purposes and in fashions that can
hardly be called artistic at all. The magic of words
is one of the strangest things in the world, and those
who use them most, often understand them least.
In our study of power we have seen what they will

do in commanding and controlling the I for practical objects. The wonder of them is no less in their high emotional excitement for rapture and delight. These little symbols, made up of fleeting sounds and insignificant impressions on the printed page, can flood the human spirit, your I or mine, with the richest ecstasy of hope and the deepest horror of despair. They can flit forth over the world with a glory of color and a splendor of passion, and again, ineptly used, they can afflict us with a horror of boredom that nothing else can equal. Their power consists not only in plain direct meanings, if there are any such, but in subtle, remote associations, which plunge far down into the unconscious and cannot be disentangled by any research or investigation of the probing intellect. They carry a dancing joy and glitter even in their mere rhythmic vibration, so that, ordered as the true artist knows how to order them, they make our souls vibrate and quiver with celestial energy and again melt away with a voluptuous enervation as enchanting as it is obscure.

The curious thing is that some spirits do not respond at all to this poetic appeal, that there are many persons, men especially, and often of high intellectual cultivation, to whom verse, even Homer

and Shakespeare, is a jingle and rhyme an annoy-
ance. The same thing is even more true of that
even more subtle and elusive art, music. And the
puzzle is that those who appreciate keenly what
would seem to be the musical elements of poetry
are sometimes quite indifferent to these very same
elements in their musical form. Not only ordinary
people are destitute of musical ear, but the great
poets are apt to find music little more than an un-
meaning noise. Wordsworth cared nothing for it.
Théophile Gautier, so exquisitely sensitive to form
and color, wrote a good deal of musical criticism;
yet he said that, while he was perfectly aware of the
difference between good music and bad, he himself
cared as little for one as for the other.[3] And in the
Goncourts' 'Journal' there is a striking passage
showing the general disregard of literary men for
musical delight.[4]

Yet, notwithstanding this widespread limitation
of musical enjoyment, there are many reasons why
music should be considered preëminently the art of
the age in which we live. That age is an age of
ignorance, as we shall have occasion to develop
more fully in the next chapter, and music is above
all the art of ignorance. This does not mean that
long study and careful thought are not required to

master the secrets of musical composition, and evidently the music of the advanced modern schools is a matter of curious scientific equipment in itself. But all the other arts require for the comprehension and appreciation of them some larger knowledge of human history and human life, such as is more and more difficult to master in our complicated modern world. Music appeals directly to the emotions and to remote, obscure, subconscious associations that are bound up with them. It is for this reason that the enjoyment is so evanescent and uncertain. If little distractions or fatigues have put us out of tune, music loses its hold upon us altogether. But when it does have full sweep and range, when our surroundings and condition have put us in the mood for it, few things carry us away with so vast, so overwhelming, a mastery, make us forget so completely the petty preoccupations of the immediate I in the larger emotional possibilities of the shadowy universe.

It is because of this adaptation to an age of ignorance, because it does not demand the higher intellectual culture which is becoming more and more impossible, that music deserves to be and seems likely to be the peculiar art of democracy and of the future. People who would care nothing for the poetry of

Dante, or the painting of Titian or Turner, may
have their souls turned upside down by the music
of Wagner or Debussy, not to speak of the flaring
glory of a military band, which can lead men's
spirits whither it will. And this democratization of
music is of course greatly enhanced by the inventions of mechanical production and most of all by
the distribution of the radio, which scatters musical
performance broadcast to millions all over the wide
world. Only it must always be emphasized that
perhaps the greatest of all musical effects are the
simplest. No excitement of opera or symphony can
surpass the spiritual disturbance produced by the
lonely, quiet singing of a hymn that sunk deep into
the soul in childhood, and the warble of a March
bluebird will touch depths of passion and melancholy and exquisite despair beyond the reach of
even Beethoven or Wagner.

This simplicity, this charm of common and trivial matters, this admirable availability, are even
more characteristic of the aspect of beauty that is
most constantly familiar to all of us, the beauty of
the natural world. It is true that here, as with
poetry, accessibility to a certain extent cheapens
and deadens, and what we see or may see every day
comes to mean little to us. Daisies are as perfect

in their beauty as orchids, but people who thrill over orchids pass daisies without seeing them. As Spenser says,

> For easy things, that may be got at will,
> Most sorts of men do set but little store.[5]

And there is profound truth in the remark of Keats about letting fair things

> Pass by unheeded as a threshold brook.[6]

Yet even threshold brooks perhaps infuse a certain magic of their murmur into very humdrum lives.

The chief outcry that is made about the beauty of nature of course concerns exceptional objects and unusual conditions. People travel thousands of miles to see a great waterfall, or a deep-cut valley, or a ponderous glacier. The feeling that enters into excursions like these is largely curiosity, and for such sightseers nature becomes merely scenery. There is always the eager desire to see a higher mountain, a wilder desert, and to establish one's superiority to others by the multitude of such sights that one can talk about.

The true delight in natural objects is far different, and is indicated in Flaubert's phrase: 'It is only commonplaces and well-known countries that have an inexhaustible beauty.'[7] If you really love nature, you love it in your own dooryard, in the endless play of the sky and clouds, which you can see daily from the same window, and yet find never the same, in the old wood walks, which perhaps you have taken from childhood, in which the birds and the flowers are drenched, saturated with childhood memories of love and hope. It is the simple elements such as these that Cowper means when he cries: 'Oh, I could spend whole days and moonlight nights in feeding upon a lovely prospect: my eyes drink the rivers as they flow.' [8]

Nature, thus regarded, in its homely, perennial beauty, is at once full of the I, since it gets its magic from all the tangled threads of memory entwined about it, and it also affords an exquisite means of oblivion and escape from the tyrannous hold of the I in daily needs. The charm, the enthralling appeal of the natural world is so great that in those who feel it most it inspires a passionate, almost despairing desire, to escape altogether, to get out of this trammelling, limiting bodily existence, to become one with winds and trees and stars, and vibrate and quiver and pulsate with inexhaustible felicity in the universal life of all things. Sometimes the desire is felt most in its impossibility of fulfilment, and the soul is merely torn with a longing to attain a unity with nature that can never be achieved. And, again, there seem to be spirits, which, to a greater or less extent, really do accomplish the ideal dissolution of their own immediate I in the outer world. This happens to the poets, through their imagination, for moments at any rate, and we have Keats: 'The setting sun will always set me to rights, or if a sparrow comes before my window, I take part in its existence and pick about the gravel.'[9] But there are others, not perhaps so creatively poets, who seem to enter into nature's life with a preoccupation so constant and intense that their own daily concerns are almost forgotten in it. Such persons were White of Selborne, or Richard Jeffries. And the supreme example of this is the Journal of Thoreau, who seems not only to live with the birds and flowers, but actually to live their life, so absorbing and unfailing is the attention and the love with which he follows and penetrates the shifting and varying glory of the external world.

III

But all this receptive delight in beauty is a small matter to the passion for creating it, and in this passion we have the I affirming itself with the ut-

most intensity. There are, as I have said, persons
who are content to enjoy beauty, and often these
persons appear to have the keenest sensibility to it;
but there are others in whom, from a very early
period, the enjoyment is inseparably intertwined
with a burning ardor to produce beauty that shall
equal or surpass that which affords them such a
wonder of delight. This ardor may be curiously
directed into different channels, with some to
painting, with some to sculpture, with some to
music, with some to working in words. In all these
different forms the ardor varies little, and it is profoundly interesting to trace the working of it and
to probe as far as possible the deeper motives that
underlie it. The motives are apparently much the
same with artists of all types, and might be studied
in any of them indifferently, but writers leave a
fuller record of their experience and hence have
usually a fuller illustrative value for our purpose.

To begin with, there is fame. The artist seeks
the assertion and recognition of his I through public
applause of his achievement. It is in the highest
degree curious to observe the attitude of artists
toward this elementary impulse. Many appear to
reject and disclaim it altogether. 'I do not care a
curse for what I write,' said Sir Walter Scott. It

was an instinctive impulse, an outpouring; but what became of it, or what men thought of it, or of him, he professed to disregard. Keats rejects and scorns the approbation of the crowd: 'The more I know what my diligence may in time probably effect, the more does my heart distend with pride and obstinacy. . . . I feel it in my power to refuse the poisonous suffrage of a public.' [10] And Flaubert makes it a matter of lofty pride and supreme self-confidence to contemn the honors and rewards that popular success bestows: 'The effort to obtain any public honor whatever seems to me an act of merely incomprehensible modesty.' [11]

Yet, in spite of the denial and rejection, the thirst to be recognized and praised is everywhere patent underneath. How else are you to know that you have achieved what you aimed at? A great soldier said, when he had been beaten: 'In my profession the test of merit is success.' For the artist, also, the test is success, mingled, inept, and inadequate as it usually is. Sometimes the desire for fame is indirect and scarcely conscious, and appears with a complication of motives: 'Care for your reputation,' says Amiel, 'not from vanity, but to protect your work and from the love of truth.' [12] Sometimes there is a frank admission that glory is a great object, if not the only one. Even the quiet and modest Cowper proclaims his ambition openly and freely: 'I am not ashamed to confess, that having commenced an author, I am most abundantly desirous to succeed as such. I have (what perhaps you little suspect me of) in my nature an infinite share of ambition.'[13] And Landor puts into the mouth of one of his characters a universal statement, which may be accepted as almost universally true: 'Never was there poet to whom the love of praise was not the first and most constant of passions.'[14]

The desire for fame shows unfortunately not only in the earnest, passionate effort to deserve it, but too often in jealousy of those who have it, or appear to have, and the noble sympathy and sense of fellowship which ought to accompany and often do accompany the worship of the same Muse, are, alas, apt to be sullied by detraction and envy.

Yet, side by side with the undying effort to attain popular success, there is the appreciation of its worthlessness, and that not only when the high grapes are sour, but even with those who seem to have reached the full fruition of their hopes. Praise is so often inappropriate and misdirected. It comes for the worst we do, while the better and more serious work is disregarded. It is so ill-judged and indiscriminate, and the unthinking public lavishes its plaudits on the trivial, the temporary, the vulgar, while high achievement obtains merely a scant and grudging approval. Cowper, who was so eager for fame, gauges it aptly, when he says: 'Alas, what is an author's popularity worth, in a world that can suffer a prostitute on one side and a pig on the other, to eclipse his brightest glories?' [15] Yet, worthless as the reward may be, most artists seek it with unfailing ardor till the end.

The love of fame alone, however, might not be a sufficient motive, and there are others, and powerful ones. There is the mere delight of diffusing beauty. Some, as I have said, are strangely content to receive. But others, who have the gift, and even some who have not, are forever impelled to extend to their fellows the magic of beauty, as they see it all about them, to interpret and reveal all the strange secrets of life with art's compelling loveliness, and seek and fling abroad that loveliness, not only in things that are on the surface lovely, and so appeal to every one, but even in things that are not. It is most curious to trace in thoughtful, analytical minds, like that of Whistler, or of Henry James, this passion for making art out of life, for transfusing the common world with the magic of beauty, and so revealing its deeper secrets even to common and indifferent eyes.

And again there is the instinct of self-expression, of extending and conveying one's I to others, which in the artist, of all types, finds media completely denied to most of us, with only our stammering speech of every day. The medium may vary. For one form of genius it is painting, for another music, for still another words. But in every form there is the effort to tell secrets, to pour out one's inmost personality, and if it were possible, to infuse it, to blend it, to dissolve it in the personality of others. In the painting of Titian or Corot, in the music of Bach or Wagner, in the poetry of Shakespeare or Shelley, under varying aspects and conditions, still, still there is the passionate impulse of the artist to reveal himself, sometimes with restraint, sometimes with abandon, but always with the greatest possible completeness. And again we have that singular fact, which every writer will more or less recognize, and to which I have already alluded in discussing the social impulse in the last chapter, the readiness that Montaigne indicates, to reveal in the marketplace secrets and inner experiences which one cannot possibly communicate in the privacy of home and to the ears that would seem best qualified to hear. It is the old, old desire, which may be said to form the basic motive of this book, and which has been well expressed by a recent writer as follows: 'What I want, what you want, what we all want, is to get out of ourselves, to share the loneliness and isolation of being shut, as on a desert island, in this one spirit world, from which there is no outlet and no escape — the voice of one crying in the wilderness, in short. Some seek to touch others by doing good, by kindness, by philanthropy, some through art, through painting, literature, music, which often seems a more perfect medium than any other. But all seek it, now casually, lightly, unconsciously, now passionate, despairing, hopeless — something more than the mere touch of hands and interchange of idle words, something which shall blend myself in yourself and perhaps both ourselves in a self deeper, vaster, grander than either mine or yours.'

And then there is the pure joy, the excitement, the rapture of creation in itself, when you are lost, absorbed, carried away by the beauty that flows out of you, with no consciousness of any ulterior object whatever, whether fame or anything else. The acme of this rapture is probably in the sense of creating human beings, imaginary characters who shall live when you are dead and forgotten, who shall glow and glitter through long ages to come with the immortal permanence that can attach only to the unreal. But the excitement comes with the out-pouring of beauty of all sorts, and while it lasts, it is perhaps one of the most intense, as it is one of the most exhausting, that the world has to bestow. Hear the account of it given by Flaubert, who had known both the rapture and the exhaustion in the highest degree: 'To-day I was man and woman both, lover and mistress at once. I was riding through a forest on an autumn afternoon under the yellow leaves, and I *was* the horses, the leaves, the wind, the words that were spoken and the red sun that made them half close their eyelids drenched with love. Is it pride or pity? Is it the idle over-flowing of an exaggerated satisfaction with one-self, or a vague and almost mystical religious emo-tion? I only know that when I have gone through these ecstasies of joy, I am tempted to put up a prayer of thankfulness to God, if I thought he could hear me.' [16] And Keats, who had gone through the same ecstasies, describes them in the same high-wrought terms: 'I know no one but you who can be fully sensible of the turmoil and anxiety, the sacrifice of all what is called comfort, the readiness to measure time by what is done and to die in six hours could plans be brought to conclusions — the looking upon the sun, the moon, the stars, the earth, and its contents — as materials to form greater things, that is to say, ethereal things — but here I am talking like a madman — greater things than our Creator himself made.' [17]

IV

The life of the creative artist is not all rapture and ecstasy. There are the days and months of patient labor, both for preparation and for perfecting. This labor differs of course with the different arts. He who would paint great pictures has to spend years in acquiring the elements, before he can begin to create at all. So with music. The successful performer has his innumerable hours of drudgery, which are not only indispensable at first, but have to be persisted in to the end. The composer must study the great creations of the past and probe all their secrets before he can attempt to parallel them with even slighter efforts of his own. On the other hand, the worker in words is too apt to think that in his art very little preparation is necessary. He is using the instruments that he was almost born to use, that he is employing daily in the commonest intercourse of life. All he has to do is to put these instruments at the service of his mighty, active thoughts, and the thing is done. Not quite perhaps. It is the fatal facility that floods us with so many poets and novelists and workers in all literary lines. It is the facility that makes the amateur poet the jest of the newspapers. But to do great work that will endure, in literature, as in music, there must be profound, persistent labor somewhere. 'I grudge no pains, so that I may be but a famous poet,' writes Cowper.[18] The pains must be taken, sooner or later, though even enormous pains do not always ensure the result.

Only the labor may be extensive or intensive. There are those who toil long patient hours, to produce a comparatively insignificant bit of work, insignificant in appearance at any rate. There are others who seem to get out their product easily and with a minimum of effort. But in these latter cases there is apt to be an immense concentration of power, and as always with such concentration, there follows a corresponding nervous fatigue and even disgust and despair.

And besides the labor, there are innumerable other difficulties and drawbacks that beset the I when it would affirm itself in beauty. Voltaire was one of the most triumphantly successful of authors; yet he said that if he had a son who wished to be a writer, he 'would wring his neck out of sheer paternal tenderness.' [19] When boys and girls write to me, saying that they are determined to pursue a literary career, and ask advice, I quote to them this saying of Voltaire, at the same time pointing out that no such saying ever deterred the born artist from his appointed task. The I will not be conquered by any such experience of others.

There are the external difficulties, for instance the interruptions and disturbances. You want solitude and seclusion with your own thoughts. You feel sure that the great work would come, if you had only leisure and quiet to achieve. But friends intrude, necessary business distracts, trifles will dissipate the intense concentration on the ideal hope. Lady Byron once looked in on Lord Byron, when he was writing verses. 'Do I interrupt?' she said. 'You do, most damnably.' It was not polite, and it led, with some other matters, to domestic dissension. But many wives, with the best meaning in the world, evoke the same state of mind, if it is not always expressed. And less important things will scatter inspiration and make it hopelessly far away. As Flaubert puts it: 'A window shade askew, a fly that buzzes, the noise of a cart passing, and my fancy is off at once.' [20] And he sums up the whole matter of disturbance in one passionate phrase: 'To accomplish anything I must have the impossibility of being disturbed, even if I wished it.' [21]

Then there are the critics, who can set up the greatest disturbance of all. Some people, the wisest, avoid and neglect them, and some laugh at them, or pretend to do so. But most feel the bite of the gnats even when it is contemned. And artists generally act on the exact reverse of the advice given in the clever French comedy: 'We should respect the critics; we should not pay the slightest attention to them, but we should respect them.' [22]

The stupidity of the critic provokes, his perfect ineptitude, his emphasis on the wrong thing and complete misunderstanding of all your aim and effort. And if his injustice stings, his justice stings even more. What he says that is kindly you discount as empty compliment. But when he lays his finger on what you know to be the weak points, you wither and shrink, and it seems as if all the creative impulse had gone out of you; for, after all, there is no criticism that really counts except the haunting, persistent criticism of yourself.

And so there are the internal difficulties, even more hampering, and certainly more inescapable, than the external. There is the utter failure of inspiration, as suggested in the extreme case of Gray: The power of achievement, he says, 'is the result (I suppose) of a certain disposition of mind, which does not depend on oneself, and which I have not felt this long time.' [23] And Gray accepted the blank in his leisured, melancholy indolence. But others are less content, and seek, and strive, and hope for the spark from heaven, until their impatience calls it down.

Or again, when you are doing your work, and doing it well enough, you are afflicted by the vast doubt as to whether it is worth doing at all. The world is full of masterpieces, which no one has time to consider or appreciate. Why should you wither your soul and blight all your capacity for common joy, laboring to give it more which it will pass by with equal contempt?

And further, you mistrust your gifts, fear that your powers may fail you, that you have done your best and last work, and that if you persist, when the inspiration is gone, you will become a laughing-stock in the end. I myself have kept at a very minor sort of literary art for thirty years, and have had a moderate success, which might seem at least sufficient to establish a certain confidence. But I never sit down at my typewriter of a morning without the haunting fear that the words will not come. For a few moments the fear is almost paralyzing, then it fades and is forgotten, and the fingers and the keys fly as fast as ever. Only, some day ——!

Also, the best and greatest artists fail, all artists do, no matter what their skill or the form of art they work in. Sometimes the failure is absolute. A man is tempted to try a new line, or a new departure in his old one. Everything goes just as wrong as in his tyro days. If he is wise, he recognizes his own failure, and throws the thing aside at once. If he is unwise, he exposes it, vainly hoping, to the world, and the world scoffs at him. In either case there is a bitter disappointment, which no philosophy can quite overcome.

And there is relative failure. No one can succeed equally always. A special work, coming at a fortunate moment, will carry away the critics and the public, and the ecstatic worker will think that he will ride upon the wave of glory forever. The next book, or picture, or symphony, perhaps even quite as good, will provoke a reaction, with criticism and contempt, and the worker will have to take his turn at despair.

All these things should make the artist give up, and wish that his father had done him the paternal kindness that Voltaire proposed. But the born artist never gives up. After one such failure the discouragement may perhaps be prostrating, paralyzing. The pen may be laid aside, as it seems, forever. After all, the sun shines, the world is full of flowers and birds and charming women. For God's sake, why slave and torment oneself to make failures? Forget it, give it up, lie in the sunshine and sleep. And this lasts a little while, a very little while. Then slowly, slowly comes again the wide flood of ambition and hope. There is no joy, no life, no existence, like that passionate fervor of creation: why should one deny it to oneself, even if it does bring disappointment and failure in its train? And the burning eager, insatiable, creative I takes for its motto the golden saying of Whistler: 'The career of an artist always begins to-morrow.'

V

As it is interesting to study the difficulties of the I in artistic creation and its persistent obstinacy in overcoming them, so it is curious to consider some aspects of the creative process. First, there is the essential, fundamental element of conception, construction, composition, so prominent in every form of art, whether painting, or music, or literature. And it is to be noted that this element of composition belongs peculiarly to the artist himself, and that the ordinary reader, or spectator, or enjoyer, is not necessarily aware of it at all. It is structure above everything that makes the interest of a symphony or of a drama; but the hearer or beholder does not stop to think of this, but simply appreciates that he is carried away or that he is bored.

Artists vary strikingly in regard to this matter of composition. There are those who take it lightly, who sketch out their work and then develop it by instinct. And again there are those who must see every step and every detail planned carefully in its proper bearing, before they begin to give the final form. Take fiction. Trollope tells us that he could not construct his stories beforehand, that he simply started with a clear conception of certain characters and then let them develop their adventures and relations as they would. On the other hand, we have such extreme instances as the novels of Wilkie Collins, which perhaps represent the last word of elaborate dove-tailing of every element of structure, so that nothing shall move or fall out of its predestined place.

As regards this element of composition in the literary form, nothing is more curious than the study of Shakespeare. Shakespeare began his work as a dramatist by making over the plays of other people. Apparently the habit so formed stuck to him always, and it rarely occurred to him to invent his plots in their entirety. He took hold of some popular play or novel, often extravagant in design and trivial in execution, then let his imagination work on it, making profound, perplexing human creatures out of mere dolls and puppets, and the result is a complicated intricacy, all the more fascinating because critical diligence is never quite able to unravel it. It is this strange process of origin and growth that makes Hamlet one of the great creative puzzles of the world.

The same variety in the tricks and methods of the creating I that affects structure, affects also the detail of artistic workmanship. There are artists who improvise, who seem to live in a perpetual, golden dream, and to weave their webs as naturally as the silkworm, in an easy, constant outflow of unfailing felicity. The extreme of these improvisers would appear to be the Spanish Lope de Vega, with his hundreds of plays, thrown off almost as lightly as he breathed. Or again, we have George Sand, or Dumas, with their scores of novels, so that Gautier said of George Sand, that she finished a story at midnight and began another at one o'clock the next morning. Expression seems to be born in these people, and words pour from them with swift audacity and current grace. As Gautier described the process in himself: 'I toss my phrases in the air, and they fall upon all fours, without my further troubling.'

And again, there are the artists who cannot take pains enough. Chadwick used to tell his pupils, when they got to working nervously over their music, 'Never finish a thing after it is done.' But to the true, careful, passionate worker, to whom only perfection is tolerable, it seems as if nothing were ever done. Every detail must be right, absolutely, finally right, or nothing has been achieved whatever. Voltaire was in some respects a rapid, an instinctive artist; yet Voltaire tells us that he spent far more time over revision than over the original draught, and he insists that poetry to endure must be absolutely flawless: 'Be sure that verses which have one of these faults will never linger in men's hearts, will not be re-read and remembered: it is

only the perfect verses that are retained and loved.'[24]
Cowper declares: 'I never suffer a line to pass till
I have made it as good as I can.' [25] And the extreme
of nicety and painstaking is surely found in Flaubert, who spent a long and laborious life in the
composition of half a dozen books, who weighed not
only the significance but the sound of every phrase,
and who insisted that there was one right word, and
only one, and that it must be found, if it took weeks
to search for it: 'I have now spent three days in
making two corrections, which will not come: the
whole day Monday, and Tuesday also, were passed
in the search for two lines.' [26]

To work so earnestly and passionately with
words, you have to worship them, to find them not
only golden toys, which weave a glittering veil of
illusion over the harsh and barren realities of life,
but also cunning and wonderful instruments, which
can call the deepest secrets out of men's souls and
pour the wildest passions into them. And again, in
considering the glorious mastery over words, and
their reciprocal mastery over the lovers of them,
there is no more curious example than Shakespeare.
Just because he had little formal education, did not
grow to the use of words in slow academic and
pedantic discipline, but heard them, caught them,

loved them, as they fell from the lips of breath-
ing, loving, hating, laughing fellow-creatures, words
seem to have had for Shakespeare a peculiarly
fascinating, inspiring, entrancing significance. Who
in the world can do with them what he did? Who
in the world can so mould them and twine them and
load them with spiritual grandeur and insinuating
grace? Who can actually create words as he does:
to *chapel*, to *inurn*, to *besing*, and hundreds of
others, wayward, unruly, astonishingly significant?
Who in all the languages of the world has such
magic as informs the lines of 'Macbeth'?

> Rather shall this my hand
> The multitudinous seas incarnadine,
> Making the green one red.

And again words played their amazing tricks with
Shakespeare, and it is curious to see how, especially
in the later plays, he 'fell for them,' as the slang
that would have delighted him has it, what oddities,
what extravagances, what tortured infelicities they
led him into.

But the most notable thing of all in these doings
of the I with Beauty is the depths behind the I, or
within it, or, if you like, beyond it, that reveal themselves with unexampled splendor in the sheer process of creation. It is the testimony of all who have

made great art and have at all analyzed the process
of making it, that something enters in and possesses
them far more than mere superficial consciousness
or effort. You sit down to your task quite hopeless,
discouraged, incapable. Then suddenly, from you
know not where, out of the depths of the sub-
conscious, out of the inherited memory of ages, the
power comes upon you, and you speak, or appear to
yourself for the moment to speak, with the tongues
of angels. There is no more perfect incarnation of
the Holy Ghost, and the poor, mortal, ephemeral I
seems to be rapt, glorified, swept beyond itself, in
an amplitude of expansion, which no words can
equal and no words can convey.

And then the external realization is passed on to
others, and the question is, how they take it; will it
succeed or fail, will it bring the enduring triumph
that it ought, or sink into lasting oblivion with the
hand that designed it? As regards this matter of
immediate public response and appreciation, there
is of course a striking difference with different types
of art. The interpretative artist, the actor, or the
musical performer, gets, or fails to get, direct recognition at once. There is no more intoxicating form
of glory than the enthusiasm of a great audience,
irresistibly and obviously carried away by the ex-

pression of beauty that you have conveyed to them,
and it may be that a few moments of triumph like
this pay for all the effort and rebuff and disappointment and failure that in nearly every case have to
precede them. On the other hand, the splendor of
the public performer's success is matched with its
brevity and the extremely fading character of the
fame that comes with it. Here to-day and gone
to-morrow is almost as true of the great actor as of
the great athlete.

The triumph of the creative artist is rarely so
direct. The painter, the composer, the poet, work
in silence and solitude. The praise that comes to
them comes usually late and slowly, it is apt to be
niggardly in measure, and especially quite out of
proportion to the pains and labor and even to the
deeper artistic quality. One form of literary creation, that of the dramatic author, is indeed more of
a nature to bring with it immediate recognition and
applause though even in this case the actor is apt
to carry off his full share. How vivid is George
Sand's account of her success in one particular instance: 'I came home escorted by the students with
shouts of "Long live George Sand! Long live
Mademoiselle La Quintinie!" ... From ten o'clock
in the morning the students were in the Place de

l'Odéon, and, during all the time the performance was going on, a compact mass, which had not been able to get in, occupied the streets near by. . . . In the theatre there were outbursts and clamors at every scene, at every instant, in spite of the presence of the whole imperial family. Indeed, they all applauded, the emperor like the others. . . . I was in the official box with the prince, the princess, Ferri, and Madame d'Abrantès. The prince clapped for thirty, leaned out of the box, and shouted at the top of his lungs. Flaubert was with us and cried like a woman.' [27]

No doubt a lot of life is lived in moments like these. But to the creative artist they can come only rarely, and his real compensation, his real satisfaction must be found in the excitement, the overwhelming ecstasy of creation itself. I do not know a more striking account of what this ecstasy is than Voltaire's story of the conception and creation of one of his tragedies. That no one now reads the tragedy or thinks of it only adds to the piquancy of the description. 'I found all that great names have that is most imposing, all that the secret religion of the ancients . . . had that was most august, most terrible, and most consoling, all the passions have of torment, the grandeurs of this world of vanity, and human misfortune of pity and despair. The subject took hold of me so furiously that I wrote the play in six days, including a little of the nights.' [28] In such a tumult does the creative artist pass an existence that outwardly may be one of the most humdrum routine, and it is in this tormenting, bewitching rapture of creative excitement that the I finds at least one mode of the affirmation and oblivion combined which it seeks with such undying ardor everywhere.

CHAPTER IV
THOUGHT AND I

I

THE functions and activities of the intelligence in the early development of human history were of course quite utilitarian and practical. Primitive man toiled and struggled with eager, crude cunning to capture his prey and to seduce his mate; and the fierce pressure of his enemies and of the destructive forces of nature left him little time or attention for the growth of abstract thought.

Yet even for immediate practical needs it gradually became evident that a wider and more varied range of investigation and consideration was beneficial. To be protected from heat and cold, to accumulate food, to develop means of defence, all these ends made it desirable to study the properties and relations of material objects, which might be turned greatly to man's advantage, or, if neglected, might tend with equal violence to his detriment. The animals might be trained to do his labor, the winds and waters might assist his toil, or be made to transport his possessions.

And so, partly with necessity and partly with

114

leisure, came the wider curiosity to know all that might be known. It was clear that every particle of acquired knowledge might somehow, some day, be put to practical use. And then, as the demands of actual need slackened, there were the days and hours to be filled up, and how could they be filled more delightfully than by the acquisition of further knowledge? It took ages indeed to develop the immense, the limitless scientific curiosity of Aristotle, but once initiated, the process was inevitable and fatal in its continuity. As Voltaire puts it, 'When a nation begins to think, you cannot stop it,'[1] and the same is true of an individual, and of the race.

Naturally at all stages, not only with the man of caves and stone implements, but with the highly developed brain of the twentieth century, the first and constant object of thinking is still practical utility and immediate need. Invention, endlessly ingenious invention, is what marks the progress of the human intellect in all periods of the world. Take a discovery so elementary that its first appearance is lost in the dark abysm of time, that of the wheel. Before that discovery all transportation must have been by human or animal labor, by water, or by the tedious and wasteful agency of the drag. The first inventor of a crude and clumsy wheel, probably derived in some way from a round log, simplified toil more than almost any one has been able to do since.

In all the progress of invention what a part the wheel has played, so that the whirring of billions of them expedites every human activity and interest to-day. And by wheels within wheels the process went on, until it seemed as if the nineteenth century, with its steam locomotion and industry, its telegraphs and telephones, its thousand other applications of energy through mechanical device, was the century of invention and practical discovery. We live in an epoch of machines. The mere agency of machines in locomotion has transformed life beyond any other material power whatever. The efficacy of this change of place in intermingling human habits and thoughts and desires and needs can hardly be overestimated. Take the application of intelligence in the invention of printing. Everything that happens in any part of the world is at once accessible to any other part. In Shakespeare's time even great events in China were not known in England for years, if ever. Now they are known the next day, and the action of the whole world is adapted to them. Take discovery in medical matters, in what concerns health. Primitive man no doubt soon came to discern that certain external agencies would benefit him when ill or injured, but we have got a long way from that elementary therapy to the complicated medical researches and treatment of the present day. And, to be sure, men still suffer, perhaps suffer in some respects more than they did a hundred thousand years ago, and perhaps the intelligence causes more suffering than it cures. But it cannot be questioned that the effort to relieve suffering has been an immense agency in the development of the intelligence. And in this direction, as in a thousand others, intelligence is still predominantly practical in its effort.

II

But no doubt at a comparatively early stage it ceased to be directly practical and began to develop the eagerly and acutely reasoned curiosity which gradually comes to deserve the name of scientific thinking. There was not only the desire to make use of the objects of the external world for one's own advantage or benefit, but to understand them, or as Wallace defined it, in connection with Darwin, 'the insatiable longing to discover the causes of the varied and complex phenomena pre-

sented by living [and all other] things.' ² More and
more men came to discover that, of all the pursuits
that have been developed to overcome the tedium
of life, none was more engrossing and more satisfying than the activity of the mind. As Voltaire
expresses it, with his eager zest for living: 'Can
you believe that I have not a moment to myself,
and that I should not think I was alive, if I had?
It is only when one is occupied that one exists.' ³

Doubtless the first, or one of the very first forms
of this curiosity is in connection with one's fellow
human beings, the multitude of purely phenomenal creatures that fill our universe, so like ourselves in appearance and outward habit, yet of
whom we know nothing whatever as to their inner
lives, except what we convey to them from our own.
The close, unfailing, prying, despairing observation
of these must have been an object of intense effort
from an early point in human history, in fact from
the very beginning, yet in all these centuries how
little progress has been made in it.

Getting at the mere facts of human action is
difficult enough. We have to be carefully trained
observers to make a reliable record of the speech and
the doings of others even for ourselves. And if our
study is to be at all complete, we have to depend

largely upon the record and report of others besides ourselves. Yet from our own experience we
know how little that record is to be relied upon.
Words are distorted and misrepresented. Actions
are interpreted according to the point of view of
the reporter; until it almost seems as if, in our effort
to get at the bare, elementary facts of human life,
we are working in a haze that it is impossible to
penetrate.

But we want far more than mere facts of speech
and action. We want motive, we want to go back
of motive to what we call character. Apparently
by the somewhat hazy word, character, we mean,
as I have elsewhere suggested, a still more hazy
combination of qualities, and these qualities, when
analyzed, turn out to be merely more or less complete generalizations of speech and action, on the
basis of which motive may be deduced and conduct, most unreliably, predicted. Thus, one or two
generous actions, or even generous words, will label
a person as generous, and one or two of the contrary will suffice to suggest, if not to establish, the
generalization, mean. All of our knowledge of the
human beings, with whom we have daily to deal,
so far as such knowledge is formal and not merely
instinctive, is based on these character generaliza-

tions. That is, on a basis of observation that is always incomplete, and often actually erroneous, we build an elaborate, fragile structure, which we call character, a structure which is at any moment liable to fail us and slip from under us, and then we think we know something about human nature and can shape our own conduct according to that knowledge.

It would seem as if the student who was dealing with material so uncertain and pursuing a goal so remote and so elusive would give up in discouragement and despair. But in the first place, we cannot give up. The knowledge of our fellows, though quite unattainable, is absolutely necessary to us. We never live really alone. Every step of our action conflicts or combines with the action of these other, shadowy I's, who are at once so far away from us, and so pressingly, intrusively at hand. We can never know their real nature, never quite probe the mystery that is behind the smiling, or frowning, or indifferent faces; yet we are compelled every moment to probe it, to build perpetually what edifice of conjecture is within our reach, under penalty of forfeiting the deepest and intensest realities of our own lives.

And with the necessity of this study of humanity,

goes always the supreme delight and fascination of it. Just because it is so difficult, and because the disentangling of motive is so subtle and so complicated, it becomes one of the most absorbing of human pursuits. Even the idle and indifferent find one of their greatest diversions in watching the play of purpose and effort about them, and in hazarding curious and inept guesses as to the nature and working of them. And the deepest and wisest of scholars and thinkers feel an inexhaustible pleasure in carrying on the same investigation. No doubt this investigation may be made in a trivial, gossiping, even a malicious spirit. But in itself it is profoundly justifiable, and perhaps the most justifiable of intellectual employments, since in studying others we are studying ourselves and fitting ourselves all the time for a larger and more perfect adjustment to life.

Hence we have such profound and subtle observers as Saint-Simon, with all the vast spectacle of the central heart of eighteenth-century France laid open before him, seizing it, clutching it, with an eagerness that seems almost like a physical greed. Or we have Sainte-Beuve, after all personal desires and delights had failed, still more and more curiously enthusiastic over the one delight that never failed, that of understanding just a little more, and a little more, of the human soul. And the deepest and most permanent value of the greatest novelists and poets lies also in this very thing, that they continually tell us secrets of human life, tell us often no doubt things that are inexact and misleading, since the infinitely delicate nature of the subject permits of nothing else, but still secrets that are of the widest revealing import for our own lives.

As we have a curious and delightful exercise of the intelligence in observation of the doings of men and women, so we have an equal delight, for somewhat different minds, in the observation of the world of things, of plants and animals and inanimate objects, in the varied range of studies which we are apt to call in the more restricted sense, science. In these studies, also, the basis is the love of observing, again the affirmation and the oblivion of the I in the endless gathering of new facts and striking and interesting discoveries. And the passion for thus observing and discovering is so intense that sometimes wealth and health and even life may be sacrificed to it.

There is an extraordinary difference in the habit of observation. Some persons seem habitually to note everything, even insignificant, that goes on about them, and these not by any means always persons who are disinclined to reflection or incapable of it. Again, there are others who are so perpetually busy with their inner world that the play and movement of the external escapes them entirely. Some persons observe one kind of external object and are quite unaware of others. But for those who have a taste for it, the observation of the natural world is undoubtedly one of the purest and most unfailing sources of pleasure, associated as it constantly is with a life of action and energy in the open air and sunlight. And as this observation becomes more and more enlightened by knowledge, the charm of it is doubled, quadrupled. The eye and ear that feel associative beauty are charmed and comforted by a mere solitary walk in the woods; but the charm is infinitely greater when every flower has a secret to tell you and every bird and insect holds out a multiplicity of revelation about the future and the past. Books like Bates's 'Naturalist on the Amazons' and Darwin's 'Journal of the Beagle Voyage' show what the delight of this external observation is, and Darwin himself not only set the highest value upon the gift of observing properly, 'I value praise for accurate observation far higher than for any other quality,' [4] but recognized the unalloyed delight that it was capable of affording: 'A naturalist's life would be a happy one if he had only to observe, and never to write.' [5]

But you note that it is 'accurate observation' that Darwin values. There is so much that is inaccurate, haphazard, incomplete, distorted by a thousand considerations quite apart from the study of the pure fact itself. There is inaccuracy in seeing, inaccuracy in reporting. The true scientist must constantly mistrust his own vision, and, alas, sometimes even more the recorded vision of others. He must hesitate at no variety and minuteness of detail that will confirm his observations and give them lasting significance and validity. He must look twice, thrice, often a score of times, to make sure that his even then necessarily tentative record is correct. And Darwin sums up this element of accuracy in the most energetic and emphatic terms: 'Accuracy is the soul of Natural History. It is hard to become accurate; he who modifies a hair's breadth will never be accurate. . . . Absolute accuracy is the hardest merit to attain, and the highest merit.' [6]

To ensure this accuracy, so essential to scientific achievement, it is evident that labor, immense labor, is requisite. The worker must be content to toil indefinitely, to leave nothing, however minute, unregarded, neglected. And his patience must be equal to his industry. Years are nothing in comparison with the desired result. Nature cares nothing for years, and why should those who study her? Processes must be taken up and followed out, through several generations, if necessary. Different researches must be carried on, side by side, and the attention must turn quietly from one to another, at long intervals, until the desired end is attained.

Then, when the observations are complete, and the facts accumulated, the scientist is ready to begin the process of reasoning from them, of indulging speculation and forming theories. It is true that the theorizing is apt to intrude at an early stage, to some extent, and this is desirable and almost necessary, since observation is better handled and guided, if there is some reasonable goal in view. Only, if the observer has an object to attain, a theory to prove, he has to be doubly on his guard, to see that the accuracy of his observation is not distorted and perverted by the desire of substantiating certain conclusions.

For reason is as treacherous and dangerous to the scientist as it is in everyday life, and we have only to consider our ordinary course of conduct to see how dangerous that is. Reason, the logically ordered arrangement of thoughts and the words representing them, is an essential agent in our daily dealings with the world, and one we can none of us dispense with. It is a brilliant, subtle, penetrating, far-reaching instrument. Instinct, unconscious, habitual, reflex processes, such as we inherit from our animal ancestors, no doubt governs the great body of our action, and so far as it goes is more reliable in its guidance than reason can be. But for all the more remote and elaborate developments of conduct we must depend upon reason, and a fertile, exhaustless, magnificent dependence it is.

Yet this cunning indispensableness of reason, and its insinuating intrusion into all our most intimate daily needs, make it all the more dangerous: it is so fertile in expedients, and so ready in a thousand ways to mislead. Infinite ingenuity is its chief characteristic, and the ingenuity may be employed in many ways besides the strict and pure pursuit of truth. If an end is to be gained, if a clear, desired end is placed before us, how limitless is the activity of reason in the effort to achieve it, and how obstinate, how almost despairing the un-

willingness to relinquish the end, even when barring obstacles of fact make it obviously unattainable. To what tricks and devices will reason resort,
how astonishingly varied are its machinations and
manipulations, in the attempt to reach the object
which it set before it at the start.

Consider some of its many varied, delightful
elements. There is analogy. How readily reason,
when hard-pressed, turns to analogy in one form
or another. These things have happened so and
so, always happen so and so. Then surely this
other thing, which so exactly resembles them, will
happen in the same fashion. But on closer scrutiny,
after the fact, it turns out that the resemblance
was not complete, and there may have been a disastrous variation in the consequence. Take another element of reason, its use of words, those
fascinating instruments which we have already
considered with wonder in other connections.
Words are the tissue of reason, to how great an
extent few of us appreciate, and words, with their
swift and cunning interchange, their subtle, charming, treacherous elusiveness, are continually playing havoc with the best of reasoning, whether in
practical daily conduct or in larger speculative
theory.

Then, always, in connection with reason, even when it appears most abstract, as in connection with everything else, we have the intruding, dominating I, and the worst of reason's dangers is the fact that it is my reason, and I am determined to pit it against yours, and in asserting its victory to assert the victory of the I that is behind it. When a theory once gets hold of us, it is inconceivable the effort we make and the ingenuity we employ to support it and sustain it, and if we wish to impart a theory to others, our surest way is to make them think that it is their own. As Joubert puts it: 'We can convince others by our own reasons, but we can persuade them only by theirs.' [7] This endless intrusion of the *parti-pris*, of prejudice, of preconceived opinion, is so subtle and so pervading that the wisest hardly ever fully appreciate the power of it. As Darwin says, in his brief, quiet fashion, 'the truth cannot penetrate a preoccupied mind.' [8]

With these dangers of the reasoning process always in his thought, the true scientist endeavors in every way to meet them and avoid them. First, he makes it his rule to try everything, so far as possible. No statement should be accepted, no theory should be employed, until it has been submitted to the hard, final test of experimental fact. Many a gorgeous speculation has held its own till the laboratory got a grip on it, and then it has vanished at a touch and been utterly forgotten. The readiness to relinquish theories which have thus failed to meet practical trial is one of the chief marks of the scientific mind. As Darwin expressed it, in his very last years, after experimenting endlessly: 'I wish that I had enough strength and spirit to commence a fresh set of experiments, and publish the results, with a full recantation of my errors when convinced of them.' [9]

Such eagerness to find one's mistakes and readiness to admit them bring recognition of the standpoint of others and a disposition to enter into their attitude even when it is different from ours. Perhaps Montaigne's statement of the matter is extreme: 'No propositions astonish me, and no beliefs disturb me, no matter how contrary they may be to my own.' [10] But certainly those get farthest who are willing instantly to give up their own theories when some one else offers a better. Such willingness is rare, perhaps in its perfection nonexistent, but it is a good ideal to aim at.

And this recognition of others' point of view, of their power to form theories quite as good, or even better than our own, brings with it tolerance, and even humility. When one has been speculating all one's life and seen the failure of one speculation after another, one may not be cured of the habit, which is probably incurable, but one at least learns to respect the right of others to a similar indulgence, and one gradually comes to have little confidence in any speculation, of one's own at any rate. One enjoys reason, revels in its infinite abundance and resource, but one gains a gradual humility as to the enduring value of its achievement.

All these virtues, patience, industry, openmindedness, tolerance, humility, may be summed up as constituting the ideal scientific spirit, and all the virtues should work together in that spirit for one unfailing object, the pursuit of truth. Truth may or may not be unattainable, but the highest function of the human intelligence is to seek it, and the I finds and feels no surer assertion of its power than in such search. Here again, we have the scientist's creed, stated by Darwin, who surely was as typical a man of science as ever lived: 'For myself I would, however, take higher ground, for I believe there exists, and I feel within me, an instinct for truth, or knowledge, or discovery, of something the same nature as the instinct of virtue, and our having

such an instinct is reason enough for scientific researches without any practical results ever ensuing
from them.' [11]

III

This high ideal of the scientific spirit applies to
all the forms of intellectual activity, but we are apt
to confine it to the study of the external world.
The questing, restless, eager energy of thought,
however, expends itself with equal ardor on the
internal world, on the relations between the two,
and on the causes of all. And this more abstract
speculation is apt to be more intense, in proportion
as it concerns itself with the more fundamental
interests of life. There are spirits that are possessed by it, haunted by it, with whom thinking
is a passion, which not only absorbs the normal
working hours, but intrudes on those that should
be devoted to rest and sleep. Some indeed take
these matters more lightly, and argue on the nature
of God as they would on a cross word puzzle, or a
game of golf. But to those who are born with the
desire to see the end of things, and to find solutions
for even the insoluble, the perpetual questioning of
the universe is far more than a diversion, it is an
engrossing pursuit. As Vauvenargues puts it: 'I

have always been obsessed by my thoughts. . . . It is not a dissipation, as you imagine, but a continual distraction and an occupation of the most vital nature, though almost always unquiet and unfruitful.' [12]

And when thought is set free from the close test of reality and fact, which the external world, in a measure affords, it seems to feel its strength, to spread its wings, and to soar widely in untrammelled freedom through fields of exploration as limitless as they are delightful. One of the most fascinating of these fields and one which seems to be magnificently definite and certain, with a certainty far beyond anything physical, is the field of mathematics, and reason has no more superb, athletic development than in these studies of mere numerical and time and space relation, which seem to lie at the bottom not only of all practical, but of all scientific research. So far as his range goes, the mathematician works with a splendid assurance, which his more material rivals can only envy.

Again, there is the field of what may be called pure scholarship, which, if it lacks the certainty of mathematics, has something of the abstract charm, and the escape from the disagreeable test of comparison with harsh material fact. I mean such intellectual preoccupation and delight as come from editing the texts of great authors and the linguistic studies therewith associated. For some minds the preparation of an ideal text of Æschylus or Shakespeare gives a life work that is as varied and as suggestive as it is absorbing.

But doubtless the most alluring of all these wide divagations of thought is the metaphysical, which seeks to probe the nature of man, and of God, and of thought itself. The variety of these investigations is as unlimited as their scope is unbounded. Vast and uncertain as they are, it is natural that their range should be largely colored by the temperament that indulges in them. Thus we have the two great extremes of optimism and pessimism, and while a great deal of theorizing lies between the two, it is easy to see how the bent of the theorizer expresses itself more or less in the drift of his conclusion. Also, though these speculations are so difficult in their nature that it is hard to treat them without a certain amount of obscurity, it sometimes seems as if for temperaments speculatively inclined the obscurity added to the charm. In no other possible field are the magic and the jugglery of words so mighty and so misleading. And there are some of us who believe that even the most difficult theorizing may be made comprehensible and tangible by a lucid and carefully clarified treatment, whereas the tendency to envelop one's conclusions in obscurity inevitably suggests that one's own thinking is the cloudy product of a more or less nebulous and unclarified brain. There is lasting value in the weighty saying of Goethe: 'Is not the world, then, full enough of riddles, without our making a riddle out of the simplest phenomena?' [13]

In this speculative region the range of theories is almost as limitless as the range of minds, and you may find one, or build one, to suit your temper, and connect yourself with it with detached indifference or mad persistency. There is monist materialism, which reduces the world of thought entirely to the world of matter, whatever the fundamental structure of the world of matter may be, and sees in the play of spiritual forces nothing but the reaction of atoms or electrons, in restless interchange. There is the crude Deism, with or without a dualistic antitype, which makes an anthropomorphic God create and sustain a subsidiary universe that came into being at his will and exists to do his pleasure. There are all the shades of immanent Deity, which informs every parcel of spirit and matter with the mysterious presence of the divine, elucidated by theological subtlety as it has developed through the centuries. There is the final idealism, as monistic as the material theory, which recognizes thought, consciousness, or unconsciousness, as the only, universal basis, in which, with endless transformation and relation, the shifting flow of phenomena evolves and develops, from eternity to eternity. And all these types of theory combine and intertwine, and every passionate, active, thinking brain constructs, with infinite ingenuity of reasoning power, a new brand, and claims it as its own.

What interests me at least is not so much the theories, but the theorizers, the men who conceive these systems, and the curious individual fashion in which they develop them and maintain them and endeavor to communicate them to others. How long and splendid is the series of intellectual giants who have pitted their brains against the secrets of the universe. To suggest only a few of the high lights. There is Plato, with his sweep of idealism and his Socratic method of enforcing it. There is the vast curiosity and analytic insight of Aristotle, whom Landor so admirably described as 'He who hath given the best definition of most things.' [14] There is Augustine, who so ingeniously interwove elaborate metaphysics with still more elaborate theology, and there are Aquinas and his fellows, who improved upon Augustine until one turns over the huge volumes of the 'Summa Theologiæ' with the feeling almost of an intellectual nightmare. Descartes and the eighteenth century took up the sequence. Kant analyzed the universe in theory to nothing, then arbitrarily set it on its feet again for the convenient purposes of practical life. Hegel, Fichte, and Schelling wove their gigantic idealist webs with an optimistic prepossession, and Schopenhauer and Hartman with an equally pessimistic bent. And the game goes on, and will go on, so long as men think inexhaustibly, and never know. And one of the very last of the gamesters, Spengler, remarks of his great predecessors, Schopenhauer and Nietzsche, that they started with a definite preconception, and then built up a huge cloud edifice of metaphysic to establish it, while all the time Spengler apparently does not realize that he himself is doing exactly the same thing. So that one is constantly reminded of the dry comment of Goethe, whom Spengler so much admires, on the philosophers of his own time: 'For twenty years now the Germans have been soaring

in the void (*transcendiren*). When they find it out,
they will be astonished at themselves.' [15] The
trouble is that one quickly finds it out in others,
but very rarely in oneself.

There are two points of view from which one may
regard this perpetual movement of philosophical
thinking. One may well maintain that it represents
a constant progress, and that each failure, or incomplete success, is simply another step in the
steady upward ascent toward final truth. Or, one
may feel that there is merely an endless play of one
subjective illusion after another, an ever-renewed
seductive hint of the final key to all the secrets,
while in reality the key is forever hidden, or perhaps more hopelessly still, does not exist and has
never existed at all. There is the continuous,
amused or exasperated, roll of philosophers; but
philosophy remains as remote and as impracticable
as ever. As one acute, if somewhat ironical observer puts it: 'I have so much respect for philosophy that I believe it exists in truth only in him
who discovers it, and that it cannot be communicated or transmitted in any way whatever.' [16]

But from the point of view of this book the main
interest is to see how the persistent, unescapable I
intrudes into even these purely speculative regions,

as well as into what would seem to be more naturally the sphere of human passion and effort. Ambition and the love of glory belong to the philosopher as much as to the artist and to the athlete. To discover truth, and to be known as the discoverer of it, are two desires so intermingled that no philosophy has yet succeeded in separating them, and long ago in classical days it was pointed out that even those thinkers who wrote with passionate ardor against the love of glory were anxious to have their names permanently affixed to their writings.

Again, the I gets into all this systematizing in the eager, insistent self-confidence with which men espouse their theories and support them. It is easy to say with Voltaire: 'None but the charlatan is certain. . . . Doubt is not agreeable, but a positive assurance is ridiculous.' [17] And we may all, in cold blood, recognize with Joubert: 'Of all monotonies that of affirmation is the worst.' [18] But humanity affirms as naturally as it breathes, and when once we adopt a theory, it gets the whole aggressive, insistent I behind it. Fontenelle in his old age was terrified at the horrible certainty that he saw everywhere about him. He would not see any less now, or ever. Men are not only confident in their own beliefs, they at once manifest that confidence and sustain it by dogmatically imposing their beliefs upon others, from which dogmatism flows the scholastic vice of pedantry and the even more serious evil of active authority, which over and over again seeks to employ force to bring home conviction to men's minds or fears, when simple, straightforward reasoning can never do it.

And the I forces itself perpetually into what should be abstract argument. The simple exchange of reasons, with the sole object of obtaining intellectual conviction, is a beautiful thing, and one of the noblest agents in the advance of truth. But, alas, how rarely does one come across it, either in the works of thinkers, or in ordinary life. Instead, there is more often the effort to overcome, by sophistry, or by pure clamor, so that the petty, enormous triumph of the fighting I takes the place of the lofty, untrammelled victory of convincing reason.

Further, the fury of argument is too often accompanied by the bitterness of actual conflict and quarrel. When men find that they cannot convince, even by reiterated noise and irritating affirmation, they are too apt to proceed to abuse, to personal insult, and in the last resort, to violence. Of all pitiable spectacles, few are more so than the wars that have been waged and the miseries that have been inflicted to enforce a philosophical or religious theory or even to maintain the foolish misunderstanding of a word.

So it would seem that in this heated and poisonous atmosphere, saturated with the self-assertion of the I, the serene beauty of the ideal scientific spirit was very far away. Yet as an ideal we need never lose sight of it, and we can always remember that there are scholars who have lived tranquilly in the serene temples of thought, as Lucretius called them, who have eschewed or forgotten all the fury of bitter dispute and violent argument, and have contented themselves with the undying effort to let the lucid shafts of truth, to use again a phrase of Lucretius, penetrate the cold, far-reaching, impenetrable depths of the unknown.

IV

Thus the curious, questing I probes and analyzes the external world, probes and analyzes the causes and secrets hidden behind the tangle of shifting phenomena, and finally, as the acme of its investigation, probes and analyzes itself. Long ago Socrates held up 'Know thyself' as the ideal of wisdom, and even before Socrates men were intensely absorbed and preoccupied with the contemplation of their own souls. To be sure, Goethe vividly states the view of protest in this matter: 'How can one learn to know oneself? Never by reflection, but through action. Seek to do your duty, and you will quickly find out what is in you.' [19] But it is not clear that Goethe followed his own precept, and the opposite attitude is strongly emphasized by a recent thinker: 'All mental therapy and hygiene may, then, be resumed in the old Greek maxim — "know thyself." And this may usefully be expanded into the maxim — Learn to understand your own nature, more especially your own motives.' [20]

With this object in view, the earlier formal psychology developed an elaborate system of theoretical faculties and qualities, all in a sense established in psychological fact, but misleading in their precise classification, and tending to impart to mental research an air of scientific exactitude to which it could by no means solidly lay claim.

Then with the external scientific investigations of the nineteenth century came the use of physiological methods, and the inward processes of the spirit were analyzed in terms of bodily condition and nervous reflexes. Further scientific activity brought about the development of Behaviorism, the study of mental states in external manifestations, these manifestations in the human subject being extensively correlated with corresponding developments in the so closely connected animal world. In contrast to this, from the internal side came the growing study and analysis of the subconscious and unconscious, and the play of forces from these vast reservoirs all through the more superficial field of conscious existence. And these researches were still further complicated by the appearance of the Freudian speculation, with its tendency to make the sex motive so strikingly significant.

With all respect for this more systematic laboratory psychology, with the highest appreciation for all it has achieved and with even more confidence in its possible achievement for the future, some of us feel that we get more profit and satisfaction from the keen and subtle study of those instinctive thinkers, who without bothering themselves too much with the terminology of the schools, have had a passionate love for the analysis of the human soul, especially their own, and an inexhaustible curiosity in pursuing it. There are, for example, the great French moralists, La Rochefoucauld, La Bruyère,

Vauvenargues, Joubert, who recorded their observations in shrewd, incisive thoughts or sayings. And with these should surely be included Sainte-Beuve, who, under the guise of literary criticism, carried on the widest and most searching study of the human heart. In turning over my carefully marked copies of his numerous volumes, as a preparation for writing this book, I have been more than ever impressed with the breadth and depth of his human insight, though, alas, also with the sadness of it.

Again, there are writers who have made a deliberate business of studying themselves. There are the writers of confessions and autobiographies, from Aurelius and Augustine through Cellini and Rousseau to the swarm of similar books in the present day. These writings are a mine of human truth. Yet their significance is somewhat vitiated by their being generally records composed long after the fact, and therefore liable to be distorted by voluntary, or still more by involuntary misrepresentation.

Far more trustworthy in this respect are the diaries and journals kept from day to day, with the actual record of the day's experience. Even in the most external of these, those that are most concerned with what the writer saw and heard and least with himself, as the journals of Greville, or Moore, or John Quincy Adams, there are extraordinary revelations, which to some of us at least form the most valuable part of the whole. And these internal revelations become even more significant with diarists like Pepys or the Goncourts, who had a gift for them.

But there is still another group of diarists, who concern themselves comparatively little with the world of external phenomena, but are almost wholly occupied with the sometimes morbid, but always intensely illuminating record of the world of experience within the I. As a matter of fact, the 'Essays' of Montaigne are practically such a record, though formalized and more subjected to literary treatment and conditions: 'I study myself more than any other topic; that is my metaphysics, and my physics.' [21] More purely direct, simple, and unadorned are the diaries of Maine de Biran, of Maurice de Guérin and his sister, of Marie Bashkirtseff, and very recently the strange, morbid record of Barbellion, in which a diseased spirit analyzes itself with extraordinary lucidity and persistency.

But of all these records the one that goes furthest in dissolving the I, in resolving it, if not in solving it, is the 'Journal' of Henri Frédéric Amiel. When Amiel has finished his dissection, analytical thought has done all it can do, and the gross, dominating, brutally aggressive I has been reduced to a shadow of a shade. With what a strange effort of language does he labor to render this transmutation and dissolution of being: 'I feel myself to be a chameleon, a kaleidoscope, a protean creature, capable of being shifted and polarized in every possible fashion, fluid, virtual, consequently latent, even in my manifestations, absent, even in my representations. I look on, as it were, at the molecular whirlpool, which is called individual life; I have perception and consciousness of this constant metamorphosis, of this irresistible flux of existence, which takes place in me; I feel all the parcels of my being fleet, renew themselves, modify themselves, all the drops of my river, all the rays that are darted from my force of individuality.' [22]

Self-analysis cannot go further. If we indeed make the I identical with the physical organization, and if we assume that all the intellectual powers have been developed to assist in the preservation of that physical I, we are here, as so often, confronted with one of those curious paradoxes, which such a view presents. For we have the reasoning power, developed essentially and precisely that the I may be preserved and sustained and emphasized, yet in the end devoting all its energy, all its subtlety, all its infinite versatility of resource, to the demolition, the dissolution, the destruction of the I, which it was intended to preserve.

And Amiel, like most of the other subjective diarists I have mentioned above, is a striking example of the morbid and diseased lengths to which the thinking process in general and self-analysis in particular may easily be carried. Abstract thinking is a magnificent intellectual exercise, but it is apt to become a tyrant, if it is indulged too much. You not only long to solve the secrets of the universe, you feel bound to solve them. You not only deal with them at appropriate hours and in suitable places. They engross, they encroach, they demand the time and strength that you should properly give to love and joy and life. In some over-sensitive spirits they take on morbid aspects almost approaching madness. In gay companies, in active pursuits, some haunting question will suddenly present itself, perhaps some petty mental intricacy, which can hardly be solved, and is not worth solving, yet the intense, brooding preoccupation with it is sufficient to cloud the noonday sun and take all the ecstasy out of existence. To such perturbed, unhappy souls thinking may easily become a disease, a disease which can only be got rid of by a systematic control of thought, the need of which is often not appreciated until it is too late. Hence arise a thousand ugly webs of what the psychologists call 'compulsive mania,' unreal and almost incomprehensible to the healthy mind, but inconceivably tormenting to those who have to undergo them.

Yet, on the other side, to those who take it more sanely, the delight and splendid resources of thinking and intellectual activity seem inexhaustible. Nothing gives the I more the sense of power, of the wide command and spiritual control, which it is always looking for, and few things so afford enduring, if not the most intense, dissipation and distraction. One who had employed these resources to the utmost loved to repeat: 'We weary of everything except to understand.' And Voltaire, who, if not a profound thinker, was one of the most keenly active ones who ever lived, puts the same thing more elaborately: 'There is delusion in everything in this world, but there is less in study than in other things: it is a supreme resource at all periods of life and it nourishes the soul even to the very end.' [23]

V

The drawback to this passionate pursuit of knowledge is the ever-present, haunting consciousness of ignorance that it brings with it. It is only those who know little or nothing who have a blissful contentment in the feeling that they know quite enough. But when thought begins to reach out, to test its powers and sweep its blurred vision over the wide world, it gradually becomes aware of how limited that vision is, and how utterly incapable of ever penetrating the dim obscurity that fills the infinite void beyond our intellectual grasp.

And if this brooding sense of ignorance has afflicted the thinker in all ages, the heavy and the weary weight of it must be far more oppressive in our own age than it has ever been before. It is not only the sense of general human ignorance, of the manifold things that humanity at large does not know and never can know. The last two centuries have made vaster inroads in all directions upon this waste of the unknown than have ever been made before, however petty the results may be, compared with the range of possibility. But it is precisely this increase in general human knowledge which makes the personal ignorance of each individual so much more profound and overwhelming. Take any, take every department of thought or investigation. See how the researches have extended, how the books have piled up. The most rapid reader, the most intense and vigorous thinker, cannot pretend to keep acquainted with even a generalized synthesis of all that has been accomplished.

The acceleration of which Henry Adams complained, superficially obvious in the world of mechanical motion, is even more obvious and crushing in this world of intellectual activity. One may try in two ways to meet it. One may endeavor to keep some grasp on the general progress and movement of thought in all lines, and in this case one is sure to get only a superficial and dilettante hold, if even that. Or one may deliberately shut oneself up in some cavernous specialty, determined to dig to the bottom in one's own line and let the rest of the world go as it will. Yet even to those who accept such an alternative satisfactory results are impossible, and the specialist is overwhelmed with printed matter in his own specialty which he can never completely master or follow. It is for this reason that I insist that we live in the great age of ignorance, and that we are smothered in the mist not only of what we cannot know, but in the more oppressive mist of what we might and should know and do not. Even in that time of assured intellectual confidence, the Middle Ages, it is said that the last dying word of one of the most learned and most confident, Abélard, was 'Je ne sais, I do not know.' Assuredly to-day it must be the first and last word of all of us, living and dying.

It is easy to emphasize the misery, the tragedy, of this state of universal personal ignorance. We grope, we flounder, we gasp, we struggle, and we vanish. In Mr. Mencken's clever study of democracy he points out that the condition of childhood as of primitive man is one of instinctive fear, and that this fear is dissipated by education. We come to understand the powers of nature and the objects of nature, and we lose our dread of them as regards the surface of things. But as the education progresses, we come to see that in reality we understand nothing whatever, and again the dense night of ignorance closes about us, and the fear returns, not with childhood wailing, but perhaps with an even greater silent shudder and despair. This subtle interrelation between fear and knowledge is delightfully indicated in the comparison between the two words *apprehension* and *comprehension*. Comprehension, entire grasp, solid, complete understanding, is sturdy, self-possessed, free from fear. Apprehension, intellectually, to perceive, to reach out for, to grope obscurely, tentatively, becomes in the emotional world, by delicate transmutation, synonymous with a vague terror.

Yet the consciousness of personal ignorance has its good side also, which for some fortunate souls seems to be the prevailing one. In the first place, it is possible to accept one's limitations with infinite serenity, if not with complete oblivion. 'Nothing puzzles me more than time and space,' said Lamb, 'and yet nothing puzzles me less, for I never think about them.' [24] And Montaigne, with his supreme practical Epicureanism, puts the thing admirably, when he says: 'It requires very little learning to know how to take life easily.' [25] One would not suspect the great Thomas Jefferson, with his somewhat doctrinaire eighteenth-century tendencies, of being too ready to confess intellectual deficiency, yet he speaks with fondness of the 'pillow of ignorance on which the head may repose comfortably as on a pillow of down.' [26] And again that universal interpreter Montaigne may have furnished Jefferson with this idea, or may not, for he says: 'Oh, what a sweet and soft and wholesome pillow are ignorance and incuriosity, to give repose to a healthy and normal head.' [27]

But besides the somewhat negative comfort of accepting ignorance serenely, there are positive benefits, of high and lasting value, that follow in the train of such accepting. The recognition of one's own personal, individual ignorance, not a proud agnosticism, insisting that no one can know, not a dogmatic scepticism, urging universal doubt, but the simple admission that I do not know, that you do not know, however great may be the wisdom of others, carries with it the two charming virtues of the scientific spirit, humility and tolerance. We are bound to be gentle with what appear mistakes in the thinking of others, when we appreciate that our own thinking is saturated with error, and it may be that a great aim of education, perhaps even the greatest aim, though an aim too often neglected, is to teach us how much we do not know.

Also, there is something to be said for meeting ignorance with the play of the comic spirit, which dissolves these vast perplexing problems by a touch of airy indifference, which views the most bewildering puzzles and the most passionate trifles alike under the aspect of eternity, and which to tolerance and humility adds the last perfecting grace of a smile. As Renan has it: 'The world is a comedy at once infernal and divine, a wild, strange dance, arranged by a leader of genius, in which good and ill, beauty and ugliness, sweep by in the place that is assigned them in view of some mysterious end.' [28]

Thus, as with beauty and power, the I at once affirms and escapes itself in thought and the adjuncts of thought, and it grows to seem as if by burying oneself in absorbing intellectual effort one might lose altogether the haunting obtrusion of the I in its petty, daily needs and preoccupations. Yet even in the soaring rapture of abstraction there is always the sense of unescapable solitude, and though you may be able to reach out beyond the milky way, you cannot by any possibility think yourself inside one of these petty, adorable human bodies which mean more to you than all the suns and stars. Moreover, when the abstraction is most intense, want and loss and misery come, or just simple toothache, for there was never yet philosopher who could endure the toothache patiently, and the I is thrown down from its airy height with a sharp, harsh thud upon its homely, hateful, narrow basis in this tormented world. So that sometimes one is tempted to compare the incomprehensible, petty I-totality to a gas or fluid, which can be dissipated in thought, as the ether is dissipated through the vast spaces of the universe, and again in an instant is condensed into one acute, minute infinity of concrete agony. Then, in the gross, engulfing flood of material disaster, one seeks some surer support than thought or beauty, some supreme divine refuge, some firmer hold upon the immediate presence and power of God. In our next chapter we will consider such a hold, so far as it is suggested in the history of Jesus.

CHAPTER V
CHRIST AND I

I

AMONG all the varied agencies for disciplining the mutinous, rebellious, all-engrossing I, none probably has been more notable or more efficient than the life and teaching of Jesus. Therefore it seems fitting, as typical of those agencies, to make the figure of Jesus and what he represents a central element and as it were the keystone, in the structure of this book.

It has often seemed to me that if it were possible, it would be a most interesting experiment to take a man of average intelligence, with average modern mental training, critical sense, and contact with the world, who had never heard of the Christian religion or anything connected with it, give him the New Testament to read, and get his fresh impression of it. Naturally no such experiment or anything really approaching it, could ever be made. Jules Lemaître says of the great literary classics: 'I am condemned never to know them because I know them too well.' So it may be said of most of us with the Bible. We have been so saturated with its language, its traditions, its viewpoint, from earliest childhood, that we can never come to it or judge it with any freshness of impression at all.

At the same time I feel that I myself am a little more in a position than a good many persons to approximate the experiment indicated above. I was indeed intimately brought up on the Bible. Its thought and its phraseology became part of my being, and its turns of expression constantly enter into my writing and speech. Yet, for reasons not necessary to detail, it happens that I have not read a chapter of the Bible continuously for over ten years, and have not read the Gospels as a whole for a great many more years than ten. It is more than twenty-five years since I went to a church service, except an occasional wedding or funeral, so that I have not even heard the Bible read in that way. In the course of those years a multiplicity of mental and moral experiences has so developed and modified my view of history and life that to take up the New Testament now and read it continuously seems like an almost unwonted adventure. For the purpose of this book such reading was necessary, and I have carried it through, aiming, so far as I could, at the obviously impossible, that is, to read it as if I were reading a life of Buddha or

Mohammed, which was utterly strange to me and narrated events and circumstances of which I knew practically nothing.

In this process of study I have confined myself to the Authorized Version of the Bible, not turning to the original text or to any commentary whatever. This version, or the revised modern substitute, is the document upon which the Christianity of the Anglo-Saxon race, in England and America and many other portions of the world, is mainly based, and it appears that by it Christianity, as a popular force with that race, will stand or fall. It must be remembered, however, that the English Bible, simply from its form, has an extraordinary, naïve, appealing beauty, which gives it an immense advantage over the merely academic translations of other religious books. Take, for example, some of the most conspicuous specimens of Eastern religion in the collection called 'Sacred Books of the East.' The translation naturally varies in quality. But in those that I am familiar with it has a halting inadequacy, a groping dumb inarticulateness, far different from the unfailing grace and magic with which the English translators clothed the Holy Scripture with which they had to deal. The unsurpassed charm of the English Bible, in all its

parts, both in its unrivalled simplicity and grandeur of phrase and in its subtle, enthralling perfection of rhythm, is like the charm of the primitive Italian painters, and this charm holds us even
when we may have lost something of our reverence
for the content.

The New Testament, at any rate the Gospels,
may be regarded as a biography of Jesus. For
twenty years my chief interest has been the biography of men and women, and it is natural that I
should apply the results of my biographical studies,
so far as possible, to the Gospel narrative. It is
hardly necessary to indicate at the outset that, like
the entirely remote observer suggested above, I
assume that the Bible is a historical document like
any other, no more infallible than any other and
subject to the same critical analysis as to veracity
and reliability as any other, and that Jesus himself
was a historical personage, to be studied in the
light of the general principles that apply to all
human conduct and motive. Biographical study,
such as I am accustomed to, would be stultified
and rendered impossible on any other assumption.

Where direct access to the person considered is
excluded, biography becomes wholly a question of
derived material, and with persons historically re-

mote, of material that is printed. Years of careful investigation and scrutiny of such material have not in the least diminished my love for humanity or my faith in its good intentions, but they have reduced my confidence in human accuracy and reliability to a fantastic minimum. I certainly should not adopt the bookplate of Sainte-Beuve's critical friend, 'Remember not to believe'; [1] but I should cling with most conservative adhesion to the Scriptural maxim: 'Prove all things; hold fast that which is good.' [2]

In my experience the one form of biographical material that counts and is to be looked for above all others is the actual written word of the subject himself. For numerous reasons even what purport to be such words cannot always be relied upon, and when we get the words, we have the process of interpretation, which is often extraordinarily difficult. Still, when we are dealing with a man's own literary productions, or letters, or journals, we have something solid and substantial at least to start with. It is needless to say that we have not one scrap of what even professes to be the actual written word of Jesus.

Far behind such personal writing in value comes the report of a man's words by others, and the most important part of the Gospel narrative is of this character. Here it should be first and solidly appreciated, how unreliable such report is at its very best. Renan asserts: 'It may be said that among the anecdotes, the discourses, the notable sayings reported by historians, there is not one that is rigorously authentic.'[3] Even careful observers and recorders of modern times err and conflict in their record, and few, if any, are entirely to be relied upon. The Goncourts prided themselves on being careful, conscientious listeners and on making immediate notes; yet the accuracy of their conversations was vehemently disputed by the persons concerned and by others. A thousand impulses of subtle and unconscious prejudice may influence the recorder to color and transform, even when he has not the least intention of doing so.

Now, leaving aside all discussion as to the chronology of the Gospels, it seems hardly likely that the words of Jesus were taken down at the moment as he uttered them. The reporters of those words were probably in the main uneducated and were certainly without any glimmering of modern habits of critical accuracy. Further, the reporters had endless prejudice and prepossession to lead them, with perfectly honest purpose, to modify and distort what they thought they had heard. Take, as an extreme example, the vitally significant words of Jesus on the Mount of Olives: 'O my Father, if this cup may not pass away from me, except I drink it, thy will be done.' [4] These words were spoken at a distance from the disciples and when they were asleep: how then could they be recorded? Take again the actual words of Deity. One would think that here at least exact accuracy was indispensable, inaccuracy unthinkable. Yet the utterance in Matthew, XVII, 5, differs from that in Mark, IX, 7, in an important particular. When points of this nature are considered, it seems impossible to place entire confidence in the reported words of Jesus in any connection.

The same is true of the narrative of facts and events. Whether the different Evangelists write from memory or from a common source, the stories they tell, while agreeing in many important elements, differ constantly in detail in a fashion not only puzzling, but such as to make one feel everywhere that one is treading on most uncertain ground. Accuracy seems apt to be subordinated to spiritual ends, for instance in the constantly obvious tendency to see that the prophecies are fulfilled at any cost. Take a minor example of variation.

In the earlier Gospels, when Jesus is arrested, the ear of the High Priest's servant is cut off in the affray. That is all that is said. But Luke, manifestly to prevent any charge of cruelty on Jesus' part, adds that he saw to it that the ear was miraculously healed. In a far more important bearing, take the narratives of the resurrection. It is most curious to see the comparatively simple and elementary story of Matthew grow gradually into the far more elaborate account of John. And in general it may be said that, while the Fourth Gospel is in many ways the most significant for the understanding of Jesus' nature and spirit, the differences between the record of John and those preceding are of a character to shake one's confidence more than anything else. The study of the other writings attributed to John, the Epistles and Revelation, is immensely helpful in understanding the Fourth Gospel, but does not tend to make one's confidence any more substantial.

In this spirit of a critical outsider let us attempt some outline of the external life of Jesus, considering the Gospels only. To begin with, we have the child born of a virgin through direct interposition of the Deity. All that need be said of this is that it is met with over and over again in history and is a common development of human imagination or delusion. Of Jesus' early years we know practically nothing, of all that hugely significant formative period, which lays the foundation of the man in the hopes or the struggles or the passions of the boy. We can conjecture a dreaming Jewish youth, deeply devoted to hearing the Scriptures and to reading them, with an imagination obsessed and fired by the prophecies of the Messiah, who should cleanse and purify the wicked world that had forgotten its God, and by its innumerable transgressions had richly merited the coming of God's appointed Judge, who should reward the righteous and condemn the evil to their deserved punishment. And with this Jewish ethical attitude, we must conjecture also an individual disposition of divine tenderness and pity and sympathy by no means so commonly associated with the Jewish prophetic type. The rare glimpses given in the Gospels, such as the discussion of the Scriptures in the Temple, are but a slight basis for even such conjectures as these.

From the time of the beginning of Jesus' actual preaching, when he was thirty years old, it may be possible for the ingenuity of commentators to construct a consistent narrative. To one who simply reads the Gospels themselves, with close attention, there appears to be a chaos of shifting scenes, of complicated incidents and discourses, of events trivial and events profoundly important shuffled together, until Jesus begins his final journey to Jerusalem, and is there arrested, haled before Pilate, who makes an ineffectual, indifferent effort to protect him, finally turned over to the fury of those who resented his preaching and his assumption of Messiahship, crucified, buried, rises from the dead, and appears at different times to different groups of his faithful followers.

The resurrection may perhaps be regarded as the crowning miracle in a long and varied list, which accompanies this complicated career. I confess, however, that in my fresh reading of the Gospels the most unpleasant and disappointing impression has come to me from the miraculous side. It is not in the least necessary to start with any *a priori* assertion that miracles never happen. Even a moderately extensive study of history teaches that all religious movements whatsoever are always accompanied by the miraculous in some form. There seems no good reason for accepting one set of these supernatural manifestations and rejecting others. Neither is it in the least necessary to assume deliberate invention or falsification. Of the various activities attributed to supernatural power in religious development some deal with obviously or possibly psychopathic cases, some are explicable by the consideration of crowd psychology, some involve individual delusion, some are honestly imagined, and some no doubt invented. But an examination of many such cases and possibilities leads one to conclude that the probability of human misrepresentation and misunderstanding, coupled with the infinite range of human credulity, is far greater than any probability that the supernatural has ever taken place. Most of all, I must repeat that in my study of the Gospels nothing seemed so much to injure, to cheapen, the effect of the story of Jesus' life and teachings as this perpetual introduction of a more or less meaningless and inappropriate thaumaturgy. Why blast an unfortunate fig-tree that was doing its best? And the miracle of the loaves and fishes, told over and over by the Evangelists with such happy complacency, serves admirably to gauge their intellectual calibre. As Sainte-Beuve says of the miracle of the Holy Thorn at the Monastery of Port-Royal: 'The Jansenists saw in it the triumph of their cause; I see in it chiefly the humiliation of the human spirit.' 5

But out of this somewhat disconcerting and unsatisfactory tangle of supernatural events there springs a perennial fountain of spiritual light and refreshment in the discourses attributed to Jesus. To appreciate fully the beauty and significance of these discourses, it is necessary to see them in their surroundings and background. There is the simple, pure outline of that Syrian landscape, with its wide reaches of country, its blue sky, its blue waters, and the snow-capped mountains in the distance. There is the audience, at first composed of humble village folk, like Jesus himself, fishermen and shepherds, simple in their pastoral traditions and habits. As his fame spreads and increases, the more or less great ones of the world begin to be added, some coming from pure curiosity, some to profit by his miraculous powers, some to carp and criticise, and a few to feel the charm and to follow the Master's footsteps everywhere. And always in the midst of them there is that simple, august, earnest figure, seeking truth and purity and love, in the hearts of childhood and in the hearts to which truth and purity and love may restore something of their childhood innocence.

Even in the discourses there is the element of incoherence and inconsistency that I have suggested earlier. Speeches that could hardly have come together are grouped with little relevance and grouped differently in the different narratives. The lack of order, of system, of definite chronological arrangement, when one dwells upon it, disturbs and confuses. After the comparatively concrete and practical tone of the earlier Gospels, the far greater refinement and elaboration of John continually set one trying to account for and explain the difference.

Yet the unique force and engaging, enthralling power of the discourses is there persistently. How pat and appropriate they are. The parables, with their intense local flavor of the Oriental apologue, how they seem to grow out of the soil, as it were, to distil the highest things of the spirit from the immediate and almost trivial involvement of circumstance, with the native gift of the born teacher and the born poet. How apt, and shrewd, and appropriate is the turn given to embarrassing or thwarting incidents or arguments. There comes the puzzle of the tribute-money, and it is met with the conclusive answer: 'Render to Cæsar the things that are Cæsar's.' [6] There is the woman taken in adultery, and the quiet comment, that has echoed over the world ever since, finding its response in hearts, if not in lives: 'He that is without sin among you, let him first cast a stone at her.' 'And they which heard it, being convicted by their own conscience, went out one by one, beginning at the eldest, even unto the last: and Jesus was left alone, and the woman standing in the midst.' [7]

Above all, there is the heavenly sweetness, the ineffable, profound spiritual insight, which without making a shadow of pretence, seems to go to the bottom of the world. There is the keen, quiet appraisal of the deepest moral truths: 'But wisdom is justified of all her children'; [8] or the inimitable, 'For the children of this world are in their generation wiser than the children of light.' [9] There is the expression of love and tenderness, of infinite pity and comfort, which the world has never seen equalled and never will, which has brought relief and hope to those who seemed utterly beyond the reach of them. 'Peace I leave with you, my peace I give unto you: not as the world giveth, give I unto you. Let not your heart be troubled, neither let it be afraid.' [10] And millions of weary hearts have listened, and have forever cast out fear. 'Come unto me, all ye that labor and are heavy laden, and I will give you rest.' [11] How many worn, sick, frail, tormented spirits have found their peace in that. 'And

168

I will give you rest.' How many who have fought the long battle and fainted in triumph or in defeat have found in those words the consolation that triumph could not yield them and that defeat could never take away. 'And I will give you rest.' Ah, if even he always could!

II

Accustomed as I am to portraying, or endeavoring to portray, the characters of men from their reported deeds and words, I find an irresistible temptation to undertake some sort of a psychograph of Jesus. With such material as alone is offered me, the task seems almost impossible. Compare Paul, for instance. More or less inauthentic and interpolated as the Epistles may be, they abound everywhere with material from which the character of the Apostle might be reliably deduced. Indeed that character seems to stand out of itself in letters of light. With Jesus all is elusive, perplexing. You think you have seized something substantial, and the next moment it is gone. Yet I cannot help seeking to evolve some orderly result from the confusing, misleading, veiling haze of conflicting reports and narratives.

As to Jesus' inner life and personal experiences

it is vain to attempt to see one's way with any clearness, the material is too utterly lacking. There is the almost complete blank as to the formative period, the development of childhood and adolescence, which is so essential. Had he near friends, and how did they influence him, or he them? Even his contact with John the Baptist is so vague as rather to perplex than to reveal. In his later active years women seem to have a profound interest for him and he for them. Was there some sympathetic maiden to whom the dreaming youth told his dreams and who sympathized with them and at least appeared to understand them? As to his family, his brothers and sisters, even his mother, the documents are in the last degree meagre, and the chief incident in regard to them is dubious in significance, though obviously related from the disciples' point of view: 'He answered and said unto him that told him, Who is my mother? And who are my brethren? and he stretched forth his hand toward his disciples, and said, Behold my mother and my brethren.' [12]

So with that seething and fermenting intellectual life, which was developing for so many years in quick and keen elaboration, no glimpse of it, no sort of substantial clue. And again the intensely growing aspiration is hidden from us, the overpowering sense that this laboring, toiling, suffering, sinning world needed a guide and a savior, that such a savior had been foreseen and predicted by the Prophets, and that Almighty God had ordained that the savior should be he.

When we come to the last years of Jesus' ministering activity, if we rely upon the narratives that have reached us, we can at least form more definite conceptions of his attitude toward the life of men about him, even if his own inner life is still obscure. And first as to the affairs of this world. I confess that what strikes me most is the utter remoteness and indifference to them, and not only indifference, but ignorance. To say that My kingdom is not of this world, is impressive; but the kingdom of this world is a vast thing, and most of us are securely and lovingly entangled in it. Take history. This little intense spiritual drama goes on in one corner of an insignificant province. Outside there is the great Roman Empire, and greater regions still. 'Render to Cæsar the things that are Cæsar's' seems but an inadequate recognition of all this. The little leaven in the long coming years may leaven the whole lump; but in the meantime I miss some apprehension and appreciation that the course of history means more than the petty unfolding of a petty tribe in Judæa.

Take again the world's practical affairs. Try to escape it as you can, Jesus' conception seems to be a simple and innocent communism, which has its charm as an ideal, but which the experience of nineteen hundred years has shown to be utterly impracticable. 'Sell all that thou hast and distribute unto the poor,' [13] 'Seek ye not what ye shall eat or what ye shall drink.' [14] These things never have been carried out, never will be, never can be. The most devoted Christians do not attempt it, but instead reason the simple principle away with exhaustless ingenuity.

And then there is the perpetual diatribe against riches, against the well-to-do and the respectable, the Pharisee and the Scribe, that is the bourgeois, the middle-class, on which the radical of to-day is waging war, precisely as Jesus was. There is the same old misapprehension, as if the world were sharply divided into rich and poor, and all the poor were sheep and all the rich were goats. Those who happen to have a few dollars have not a monopoly of all the vices, and never have had. Yet that broad and heavenly tolerance seems to fly in pieces at the sight of a Pharisee. Perhaps the Pharisees were not all sinners and the disciples not all saints. The violence of the attitude suggests, as with the modern radical, a good deal of ignorance of actual conditions, and, if one dares to suggest it, also as with the modern radical, even a trifle of jealousy, perhaps not for oneself, but for those whom one represents.

What disheartens me still more, as to the affairs of this world, is that this Christian ideal omits the things that, to me, mean most and are often what makes this world really worth while. In studying Jesus' great nineteenth-century follower, D. L. Moody, I was impressed and oppressed with the complete absence in Moody's life and interest of beauty, of æsthetic emotion, and of intellectual curiosity, of the abstract passion for truth. Even in my most active days these things, for me, made up a very large part of life, and in later years they make the whole of it. In the New Testament they do not exist, or exist simply to be reprehended and branded as in the direct road to hell. Such a narrowing of life, such a close and strict limitation, which rules out the world of Shakespeare and Kant, the world of Wagner and Darwin, I resent and resist to the death. And although Jesus' reported words suggest a delicate sense of natural beauty, I cannot see that in his conception of life the world of Greek art or the world of Aristotle's thought finds any more place than in the conception of Moody. Most of all do I miss the golden grace of laughter. Laughter may be hard and selfish and cruel. It may also be, and in its ideal is, the sweetest and gentlest agent of tolerance and kindliness, dissolving grief and rancor and fear and misery away. Now I am not aware that in the New Testament there is a smile.

In my reading of the Gospels I had one strange and illuminating experience, one of those contrasts that make the zest and piquancy of life. I passed a whole morning reading the Gospel of John, that highest incarnation of Christian love, with absorbed and passionate interest and ardor. In the afternoon I went to a musical comedy of the day, eminently of the day. There was not a touch of depth or permanence in it. In a sense it reeked with infinite vulgarity. The women were half naked, painted, bedizened in every way to arouse and stimulate the senses. The men might have been drunken and vicious. They looked it at any rate. Yet I found in the thing an unutterable charm: the suggestion of the music, the grace of the movement, the bewildering richness of the light and color, all entranced

me, bewitched me, with the intoxicating possibilities of the senses and the joy of this world. And all
the time in the background was the Gospel of John,
which has no place for these things. I could not
help thinking that the Gospel of John was written
nineteen hundred years ago, and still these things
go on, with the mad fervor that they had then. I
could not help thinking also that these painted,
bedizened creatures were perhaps, after all, simple,
innocent souls, with good and evil mingled in them,
like the Scribes and Pharisees, and like you and me.
And that it was better to smile at them than to
empty vials of wrath.

So it seems that Jesus' concern with this world is
mainly in matters of morals and conduct, and the
constant emphasis on sin and sinners impresses me
unpleasantly, as it does with Moody and the violent
forms of later religion. No doubt sin is important
enough, but getting rid of it is mainly negative. It
all takes me back to the puzzle that I used to feel
years ago over Matthew Arnold's weary reiteration
that 'conduct is three fourths of human life.' There
is some sophistry, or at least misunderstanding,
here. In one sense it may justly be said that health
is nine tenths of human life; yet the normal healthy
person takes health for granted and makes it merely

the negative basis of effort and interest. Just so
with conduct: it is vital, essential, make it three
fourths of life, if you like. But the most important
part of it is negative, what we shall abstain from,
and you cannot build life satisfactorily on a negative. The ideal, that we should all live for others,
when pushed to its logical conclusion, proves its
absurdity, and the commandments of the Old
Testament are a vehemently stressed negative,
thou shalt not, not, not!

The supreme genius and singular profound spiritual insight of Jesus showed in his transforming
this ancient negative with one divine, creative
touch, the touch of love. The commandments were
to be summed up in loving God and loving our
neighbors as ourselves. 'Love your enemies, do
good to them which hate you, bless them that curse
you, and pray for them which despitefully use
you.'[15] The world had never heard that note before, and often as it has heard it since, it has yet to
act upon it perfectly. All that could be done to turn
the negative into positive this divine transfusion of
love was able to accomplish, and did accomplish.
Yet still I find sin too largely everywhere, and still
sin does not greatly interest me as a watchword of
life, or when it is identified with some of the things

that interest me most, I rebel against the perpetual branding of it.

When we turn from this world to the other, the same suggestion of the negative is not wholly absent. There is always salvation, as Moody saw it eighteen hundred years later, and what is salvation but negative through and through? Hell is vivid, concrete, an intensely practical matter, with all its damnation, its wailing and gnashing of teeth. Heaven is vaguer, perhaps a sitting upon thrones and singing of hymns in glory, but mainly the absence, the negation of many of the things that make this world uncomfortable. When one reads the rather lurid outpourings of the author of Revelation, one is profoundly grateful to Jesus and to Paul for leaving so much of the celestial future to the imagination.

But it seems to me that an unprejudiced reader of the Gospels will be inclined to gather that, like the author of Revelation, Jesus was firmly convinced of the not long delayed coming of the Son of Man here upon earth, when the final judgment should be made and the righteous should depart into everlasting bliss and the wicked into equally everlasting condemnation and torment. Yet here also, beside these not wholly convincing forecasts, there is always the spiritual touch, before which pretension and denunciation alike seem to vanish and wither away. 'The kingdom of God is within you.' [16] 'Except ye . . . become as little children, ye shall not enter into the kingdom of heaven.'[17] Simple words of penetrating truth like those make all the apocalyptic visions empty enough.

Yet again in the treatment of God there is, if not the negative, at least the extremely practical and concrete. The God of Jesus appears to me mainly the anthropomorphic deity of the Jews and the Old Testament, and this conception, however trans-figured by love, has little impress of the pantheistic universality that appeals to the Aryan mind. Now it cannot be denied that to the twentieth century, coming after Copernicus and Darwin, anything of the nature of an anthropomorphic deity is very far away. A God who has created this earth to be the centre of the universe and man to be the centre of this earth and therefore of the universe also, who watches man's conduct with jealous care and re-wards and punishes him after the standard of a human parent — it seems evident that this was the conception of Jesus, yet this conception cannot appeal to most of us with very vital reality. Nor can it be said that in Jesus' attitude toward God there is much of the element of mysticism, as one comes to know it later in the writings of the most passionate Christians. The working out in this connection is curious: Jesus being himself the Deity, naturally dwells little upon the feelings of mystical adoration with which deity inspires him, and in dealing with mankind his view is turned rather from God, whom he represents, and toward those for whom he is laboring. The beloved Apostle does, indeed, appear to sum up his Master's spiritual religion in the phrase, 'God is love'; but the most significant commentary on this and the one that gives the key to the whole matter is the sentence that follows: 'Herein is love, not that we loved God, but that he loved us, and sent his Son to be the propitiation for our sins.' [18] There is a long process of development from this utterance to the passionate absorption in God of the 'Imitation' and of Fénelon. It is to this lack of the mystical viewpoint in Jesus personally, even more than to the general unreliability of documentary material, that I trace the complete absence of any discussion of Jesus in James's vast study of Religious Experience. It may be that reverence entered in, but it seems hardly likely with James, and one would have thought that Jesus and his sayings and his attitude would necessarily have been a central element in James's theme.

The most concrete feature in Jesus' conception of God, and what later grew to be the central and, as it seems to some of us, the essential feature of Christian doctrine, is that God so designed the world that all men were utterly and hopelessly destined to destruction, unless his Son, sent by him to be a Messiah and savior, should take upon him all men's sins and by his own voluntary suffering and sacrifice should atone for human sin and make salvation possible for all those who accepted it through him. This doctrine is of course not exposed as a matter of extensive, logical elaboration anywhere in the Gospels or in the words of Jesus; but there can be no doubt that Jesus accepted it, that he looked upon himself as expressly sent from God to redeem an erring world, and that he prepared and submitted himself for sacrifice in the full confidence that what he was doing could be done by him only and would result in a consummation of infinite glory and splendor.

The supremely interesting point here is Jesus' view of his relation to God. And as to this above all we must remember the unreliability of the documents. We must remember that the reporters were under an immense obsession that inclined them to modify, to alter, to add words that would tend to support their own increasing belief, and this is especially the case when we consider the marked difference between the Fourth Gospel and those that precede it. We must remember further, for example, that we assume that words attributed to Jesus after the resurrection cannot have been uttered under those circumstances, and must have been spoken earlier, if at all, and transferred to a later period.

Yet with all these reserves it can hardly be questioned that Jesus was himself convinced of his identity with God in a peculiar way. 'Before Abraham was I am.' [19] 'I am the resurrection and the life.' [20] 'I and my Father are one.' [21] 'Neither knoweth any man the Father save the Son and he to whomsoever the Son will reveal him.' [22] It is true that there are breaks and concessions and inconsistencies, which are perfectly explicable when one knows even a very little of the human heart. It is true that the constant assumption of the divine sonship of all men makes an easy transition to the peculiar Sonship of one. There is no difficulty whatever in understanding and reconciling such things as Mark x, 18: 'Why callest thou me good? there is none good but one, that is God.' The sense of the human nature in intimate mingling with the divine is everywhere present. Yet it appears to me difficult not to recognize as Jesus' central belief, that the Omnipotent God was especially embodied and manifested in himself.

This manifestation was of course always and at all times connected with his supreme mission; the divine love and mercy were incarnated in him for the salvation of the world. Here also there are the breaks, most notable of all the tremendous words uttered in the last agony upon the cross: 'My God, my God, why hast thou forsaken me?' [23] And it is to be observed that no words in the whole New Testament commend themselves more for absolute veracity, since the reporters here could have no possible inducement to invent, but on the contrary every possible inducement to modify or to obliterate altogether, to such an extent that in the two later Evangelists the utterance is entirely eliminated. But the weakness of sheer agonized prostration may be disregarded in the full luminous assurance which elsewhere makes itself so abundantly manifest, and there can be little question but that Jesus' own attitude is summed up in the words of John: 'For God so loved the world that he gave his only begotten Son, that whosoever believeth in him should not perish but have everlasting life.' [24]

So I conclude this hasty summary of purely personal impressions in going through what has been a strange and wonderful experience. It is evident enough that my study has been neither critical nor scholarly, but one of such purely personal impression alone. Yet even so, how utterly impossible it has been to catch the fleeting impressions, as they passed over me, subtle and complicated and completely beyond disentanglement as the minute wavelets that intertwine and intercircle on water in a rippling breeze. There was the momentary, inherited, shuddering fear of hell. There was the strange, ghastly sense of loss, as of something gone out of life, when I found the story too impossible. There was the dim and shadowy remoteness of the whole thing from this sheer material world of sunshine, and passion, and misery, which glows and surges about me. I have made a desperate effort to render and convey something of all this, but my success has been far, far from my wishes and hopes.

III

'God so loved the world.' What world? The little world of the Jews, or the wider world beyond?

It is evident that Jesus' prime interest was in his
own people, to whom the prophecies had been given
and the supreme dominion promised. Yet it is also
evident that he had whisperings and glimmerings of
a far wider salvation, for all sinners who had ever
been born, and this most of all when he found his
own people unresponsive and obdurate: 'Therefore
I say unto you, The kingdom of God shall be taken
from you, and given to a nation bringing forth the
fruits thereof.' [25]

Yet the real impetus which swept the doctrine of
salvation by Christ crucified far beyond the limits
of Jerusalem came through Paul. Perhaps Spengler
puts it a little too strongly, but he gets the point:
'Primitive Christianity was a *Magian* religion and
the soul of its Founder was utterly incapable of this
brutal [missionary] activity without tact or depth.
... Jesus had drawn unto himself fishermen and
peasants. Paul devoted himself to the market-
places of the great cities and the megalopolitan
form of propaganda.' [26] It was the fiery, aggressive
ardor of Paul, with its basis of Jewish passion,
touched with Greek subtlety, and intimately
blended with Roman tenacity of purpose, that
turned Christianity from a tribal schism into a
world religion of unequalled persistence and in-

comparable encroaching, engrossing power. Renan even goes so far as to say: 'If Paul had met Jesus in the flesh, it may be doubted whether he would have attached himself to him. Paul's doctrine is his own, not that of Jesus, the revelations of which he was so proud were the offspring of his own brain.' [27] This seems wholly unjust. The central doctrine of Christ crucified was that of Jesus as it was that of John. Paul may have amplified it, developed it, given it the universal currency of his quick and subtle thoughts and his fiery, magnificent words. Yet he was in all things a follower, not a creator, and he knew it to be so.

Then there came the formative centuries. The martyrs bled and died for the faith that was in them, thus continuing, as Jesus had begun, to give that faith the secure, imperishable foundation of suffering and sacrifice. And as the martyrs cherished it by action, so the thinkers and the talkers, with the fertility of their kind, cherished it by the infinite outlay of logical ingenuity and the fervid display of too often misplaced eloquence. Learned fathers battled with each other over intangible distinctions, which would have perplexed Jesus as much as any one else, except that he would have found unerringly the one divine simple touch that cleared them all away. Solemn councils, by mere force of numbers, framed creeds which should ensure salvation or damnation, and branded as hopeless heretics all who disagreed with them. Yet the heretics grew and flourished, and only proved over and over again that it is heresy that makes the world go on.

With the downfall of the Western Empire, the Roman Church began to develop the extraordinary organization which grew to be one of the greatest spiritual forces ever known. An unmarried priesthood, absolutely subordinate to the central authority, and concentrating its obedient effort on the advancement and aggrandizement of its own order everywhere, spread the Gospel of Christ and the grandeur of the Church through all lands and among all peoples. In the darkness and chaos of the Barbarian invasions and the first struggling beginnings of the modern world this ecclesiastical ministration was invaluable. It kept men's thoughts on higher things than their own misery and made the everlasting glory of the future shine clear through the gloom and the terror of the present. Obviously also, being human, this organization of the Church hierarchy had its human defects, and the whiteness of the Gospel light grew to be sullied by worldly ambition, by the moral disorders attendant upon an unnatural manner of living, by all sorts of intrigue and the intrusion of the unseemly habits and aims and methods of this sordid world.

As the Church organization developed into a mighty and magnificent fabric, so with the coming of comparative mediæval order and the establishment of mediæval education, the Church theology spun a web of infinite tenuity and subtlety and complicated fineness. Profound and ingenious thinkers, like Aquinas and Scotus, grafted the philosophy of Aristotle upon the speculations and distinctions of Augustine and the other Fathers, as these were grafted upon the simpler, yet in itself sufficiently complicated, tissue of the New Testament, and produced a result which some admire and some despise, and but few understand, and which may be, if not comprehended, at least apprehended dimly and afar off by the lay reader in the intricate splendors of Dante's 'Paradiso.' What strikes an outsider as most curious in all this theological development is the emphasis upon belief. Doing will not save you. No effort at mere impossible virtue will save you. Simply declare and avow your belief in some mysterious talisman, the authority of the

Church, the doctrine of the New Testament, the redeeming sacrifice of Christ, and you are saved. As we find Moody proclaiming, only fifty years ago, that 'unbelief is the crying sin of the world.'

To simple minds it seems incomprehensible that belief, which appears not to be at all a matter of the will, and in any case is so misleading and intangible, should be given such an enormous efficacy. Yet, the more one reflects upon this, the more one understands it, especially in the light of Darwin's simple, suggestive sentence: 'What an inexplicable frame of mind is that of belief.'[28] It is so desperately hard to make over one's conduct, to live the perfect life and cast one's sins and weaknesses behind one. Then along comes an infallible guide, and murmurs, only say you believe, only recognize me, my teaching, my guidance as all you need, and your sins will be washed away. And it turns out that belief is above all a matter of the will, that mankind easily believe what they wish, and to say and to think you accept the doctrine that will save you is the smoothest and the most delightful road to eternal salvation.

With the profound, illogical wisdom that has always distinguished it, the Catholic Church held that the lay believer need not trouble himself with abstruse doctrines. Let him only believe in the Church itself, and all the rest would be done for him. Protestantism, rebelling against Catholic domination in other respects, rebelled chiefly in this: if the believer was to be saved, he must do his own thinking, and the principle of salvation must commend itself to his own judgment, if it was to be operative at all. It appears to some of us that Protestantism, in adopting this view, opened at the very start the road that led to its destruction. If each individual was to be his own guide, was to deal directly with Christ alone, where was the need of a church at all? Nor would there have been such need, except that the infinite gregariousness and social instinct of humanity overrode the element of doctrine and kept the church together, though the seeds of disintegration were in it from the start. A minor phase of the same matter is the perfectly logical Protestant insistence upon the sermon, as against the Catholic emphasis on ritual. The sermon, in the hands of a great preacher, is one of the most powerful of spiritual instruments. Unfortunately there have always been many ministers and few great preachers, and the disintegration of Protestant congregations has been expedited by this fact more than by anything else.

Thus, it seems, again to the complete outsider, that the Catholic Church, with its wonderful power of recuperation, has far the best chance of being the form of Christianity that will be alive five hundred years hence, if any is. Again and again the Church has seemed on the edge of destruction. A hundred and fifty years ago Frederick the Great wrote of it: 'Nothing but a miracle can resuscitate the Church: a terrible stroke of apoplexy has overcome it.' [29] Yet the Church to-day flourishes with unabated, or even increased vigor, all over the globe. I have a friend, who, when I urge this prospect of a great future of the Catholic Church even in the United States, answers me as follows: 'It may be so; but to me, as to most average Protestant Americans, there seem to be three insuperable objections to Catholicism, three elements which seem to be vital to it, and to which few Protestants American born could ever reconcile themselves: a celibate clergy, an allegiance to an earthly power which claims at any time to supersede one's allegiance to one's own country, whenever the two come into conflict, and a rooted, indomitable opposition to freedom of intellectual activity. Can you separate these things from the Catholic Church, and can it ever regain its world domination, so long as it insists upon them?' I can only admit that these three things seem fundamentally Catholic, yet at the same time reiterate my belief in the extraordinary power of adaptation that has enabled the Church in the past to survive the most shattering blows and that seems capable of giving it a future of unpredictable power and glory.

When one surveys the vast ecclesiastical and theological fabric of later Christianity, one is naturally tempted to ask what Jesus would think of it all. It seems as if that simple, earnest, passionate Galilean spirit would be overcome with bewildered stupefaction. Yet no doubt he would find, as in the beginning, pure, innocent, lofty, devoted souls, ready to cast away all thought of this world and do his bidding. And, as in the beginning, he would find also pride, greed, ambition, cruelty, and lust. And these latter might seem so swollen and so abundant that the Scribes and Pharisees and the money-changers in the Temple by comparison would have the harmlessness of doves, though very far from the wisdom of the serpent. Within the first fifteen minutes he would be busily knotting his scourge.[30] Within the second he would lay it aside as hopelessly inadequate.

And in the same fashion one wonders what the

world of to-day would say to him. No doubt it would receive him exactly as it did before. He might come unto his own, and even the majority of his own would know him not. He would preach upon the street-corners, and the hurrying crowd would stare, in gaping indifference. The half-naked girls would paint and powder, the journalists woul(be curious, the politicians would be polite, the me of business would be busy, and the priests woul. hide him or explain him away as they have always done. As Renan puts it: 'If the views received in our day were followed, there is not a prophet, not an apostle, not a saint who would not be shut up in a madhouse.' [31]

So we come back to the theme of our book, in the appreciation that this immense Christian structure has all been developed and maintained for the controlling, the guiding, the subduing, the overcoming of the I. For twenty centuries this fierce, magnificent, dramatic struggle has been going on, and still the I obtrudes everywhere its unconquerable, indestructible predominance. As it was expressed, succinctly, not so very many years ago: 'Anyway, I am no Christian. I have no self to lose. A man who has no self cannot be a Christian, because Christianity consists in losing just that self. What a pity that no man who had a self ever yet succeeded in losing it.'

The strange, the pitiful, yet the infinitely natural and human thing, is the unfailing intrusion of the I into the very heart of this vast machine which is constructed to eliminate it. And in the best of the Church's effort one does not have to look too closely to discern the I asserting itself in pride, in jealousy, in eager ambition and the indomitable desire to perpetuate its own triumph and achievement. And this is not the complaint of external hostile critics alone. There is the despairing cry of Paul: 'For all seek their own, not the things which are Jesus Christ's.' [32] There is the murmur of the author of the 'Imitation' many centuries later: 'Multi occulte seipsos quærunt in rebus quæ agunt, et nesciunt.' [33] 'Many seek themselves in what they do, and know it not.' Nay, even in the primal words of Jesus the cunning I lurks still. 'He that findeth his life shall lose it, and he that loseth his life for my sake shall find it.' [34] That is, the I is lost but to be found again, and duty is done for its reward. The highest commandment of all does but enjoin that we should love our neighbors *as* ourselves. Alas, how very few attain even this pitch of self-abnegation!

LIFE AND I

Nevertheless, the religion of Christ must be counted supreme, at any rate for us, among the agencies that do battle with the I. As such let us deal with it more amply and analytically in the chapters that follow.

CHAPTER VI
CHRIST AND NOT–I
I

THERE are few persons who live or can live in the immediate satisfaction of the I, in the enjoyment of those sensual, or æsthetic, or intellectual pleasures, which are momentarily contenting in the actual indulgence. There are indeed some rare spirits who are so situated that they can largely enjoy these pleasures and are so tempered that they can relish them lightly, moderately, exquisitely, without satiety and without disgust, can accept them as they arrive in casual sequence and see them depart rather with a smile than a sigh. We even sometimes feel that the joyous youth of the Greek race was a certain approach to realizing this ideal. But in most human hearts, to-day at any rate, the power of prevision, of preparation, of anticipation, is so highly developed that it is difficult to be content with the present moment, even when it is surcharged with delight. Such delight is apt to trail satiety forever at its heels, and the cloudy preoccupation of the future casts a shade over the present, however sweet. Thus, the first lesson of life and the

first step in education, even instinctive, is to overcome the I in its immediate satisfactions and needs
with a view to some possibility or requisition of the
days and years to come.

This denial of the I in present pleasure is of
course first prominent, and perhaps most prominent
in connection with selfish ends. The wise quickly
learn to look beyond the mere indulgence of the
hour, and to eschew it altogether in view of future
indulgence that shall be richer, more varied, and
more lasting. Then there comes further denial for
the mere purpose of protection, saving of strength,
saving of resources, saving of money, to ensure not
only enjoyment, but simple comfort and absence
of suffering with the approach of age and weakness.
This habit and anxiety of far-sighted protection
may become so insistent that all immediate enjoyment is lost in it, and the climax of such an attitude
is summed up in the remark of a friend of mine, who
had cultivated it for years, that 'the ideal of life is
to be able to have anything you want and not to
want anything whatever,' or, as the acquaintance
of Madame Du Deffand observed, with bitter,
vivid irony: 'Yes, I am happy, as happy as if I were
dead.' [1] For the penalty of such absorption in a
purely protective and negative selfishness is that

life gradually turns into a mere desert of devastating *ennui*.

But besides this denial of the immediate I for selfish ends, there is the denial for the larger interests and purposes of humanity. Immediate pleasures and satisfactions of our own may be put aside and forgotten for the pleasures of those about us, or even to banish or diminish their pains, and some lives are nothing but a succession of petty daily privations and sacrifices, simply that others may enjoy, often with little appreciation of all that is endured for their enjoyment. And again, there is the denial of the I for great causes, though still for causes of this world. There is patriotism and political effort, there is sociological struggle and combined progressive conception. Those who get interested in general activities like these, put the immediate, temporary satisfaction of the more superficial I under their feet and forget it with an overwhelming oblivion.

II

Then there is the denial of the immediate I and its indulgences with a view to another world, to that perpetual, haunting problem of death, with all its possibilities, against which we can do so little to protect ourselves, because we understand so little what the possibilities are. In other words, there is the attitude of the I towards questions of morals and religion.

To-day a very large part of mankind flatter themselves that these questions have no longer any mystical aspect at all. The moral life is the wise life, the expedient life, and we live it, when we do, simply because it pays to do so. It is assumed that education will teach us all this great lesson. What used to be known as sins are now seen as mere mistakes, and supposed to be avoided as such. Conscience, in so far as it is profitable, becomes synonymous with common-sense, and its more exaggerated, fantastic forms are set down as a morbid condition of the nerves. Yet, for all our common-sense, there is an inherited sting that somehow pricks when we do what our forefathers called plain wrong, and Dostoyevsky's terrible story, 'Crime and Punishment,' with its scientifically educated hero, who puts a hateful old woman out of the way that he may live his life with her money, and suffers the bitterest anguish of remorse afterwards, may be regarded as typical of the complications in which the modern idea of expedient morals may sometimes result.

For century upon century sin has played an enormous part in the world. The saints have recognized it, reviled it, condemned it, have pointed out its enthralling horror in others, and bewailed its still more evident and smothering tyranny in themselves. How far away we are, or think we are, from the attitude of Jonathan Edwards: 'When others have expressed the sense they have had of their own wickedness by saying that it seemed to them they were as bad as the devil himself, I thought their expression seemed exceedingly faint and feeble to represent my wickedness.' [2] And this attitude of self-condemnation, of self-despair, is magnificently summed up in Pascal's: 'The true and sole virtue is to hate oneself.' [3] We think we have shaken off all this. We think we view life more wisely and more sanely than did Edwards and Pascal, not to speak of Jesus. Perhaps we have lost as well as gained, and it may be that sin, like some other things, is not quite dead yet.

Also, there is not only the consciousness of sin in this world, there is that mysterious other world, with all those disquieting possibilities. The agreeable possibilities, reward, delight, heaven, we will leave for another chapter. Here we are concerned with hell, what there is left of it. The same persons who have turned sin into a mistake and the moral law into a wise expediency, are inclined to think that they have disposed of hell forever. Even for those who are less optimistic it does not seem as if a material hell could have quite the hold it used to have, considering how science and the growth of knowledge have probed and mapped the universe, leaving no physical lurking-place for any such concrete storehouse of the damned as Dante depicted with his vivid imagination of horror. We are taught somewhat vaguely that sin carries its own torment with it, and the self-indulgent, the licentious, the cruel, and all the rest, including very likely you and me, are contriving a more or less permanent punishment for themselves more poignant than even Dante's imagination could conceive. But the teaching is so genial that it hardly comes home to us with any great force of compelling atrocity.

In fact, hell has become so shadowy, that it is hard to realize the mighty and terrible instrument that it used to be, for stirring, perplexing, harrowing, the souls of men. Two hundred years ago Jonathan Edwards stood in his pulpit and flung such horrors as these at his awed congregation: 'That world of misery, that lake of burning brimstone is extended abroad under you. There is the dreadful pit of the glowing flames of the wrath of God; there is hell's wide gaping mouth open; and you have nothing to stand upon nor anything to take hold of; there is nothing between you and hell but the air; it is only the mere pleasure of God that holds you up.' [4] These things were not only proclaimed by men to strong and healthy men. They were served out to women and delicate children as their daily diet, and Mary Lyon stood up in her chapel at Mount Holyoke, before the sensitive girls who had been entrusted to her care, and 'would uncover the fiery billows rolling below, in the natural but low, deep tones with which men talk of their wills, their coffins, and their graves.' [5] It was not only the ignorant and foolish who were penetrated with such conceptions. Edwards and Mary Lyon had minds as well stored and largely disciplined as any of their time; and an intellect so high and finely trained as that of the poet Cowper could pass a whole life brooding over the eternal condemnation from which he saw no refuge and no escape.

The world may be better off without these things, but there was a time when they were very real and overwhelming, and even now perhaps they have not vanished, at least in their shadows and reflections, as much as we should like to suppose. We all have endless possibilities of hell in our bodies and in our souls, and so long as this is so, we can never quite escape the dread of it. We all see death before us, with its plunge into the gulf of the utterly unknown, and however we may laugh or trifle or endeavor to forget, or rush hither and thither, in agitated fury, the dread of death has a quiet, cold, nestling corner in the hearts of every one of us.

We are the children of fear. We battle with it, we slight it, we think we have overcome it, but fear is an essential condition of our lives, the most efficient and constant agent of that instinct of self-preservation which appears to be the deepest root of our being. And fear, in its derivative forms of prevision and protection, is so apt to overshadow immediate delight, that in sensitive temperaments and curiously developed imaginations and intellects, it dulls even the capacity for such delight, till life becomes a burden and a weariness. Hence spring the thousand forms of pessimism, satiety, disgust, until death, with all its horror and uncertainty, takes on the aspect of comforting release. It is not the poor, or the struggling, or the externally unhappy, who alone proclaim the misery of our earthly existence. It is quite as often those who would seem to have the happiest lot, who have tasted all the varied pleasure and satisfaction that life has to give, and who have come to see the emptiness and bitterness of it. It is the great preacher, the profound thinker, the mighty poet, John Donne, who cries out, 'Man has no centre but misery.' It is the well-born, rich, successful authors, the Goncourts, who murmur, 'Life is a nightmare between two nothings.' And Voltaire, to whom this world would seem to have offered every gift, and who relished those gifts to the full, yet confides to a friend: 'I think myself the happiest of men; but I must not mention it: it would be too cruel to the rest of mankind.' [6] While Voltaire's general comment on life is: 'The end of it is dreary, the middle is worthless, and the commencement is ridiculous.' [7] No doubt there are many who never take this tone, no doubt most of us avoid it when we can. But the great problem of death is there just the same, with all it may carry with it, and we do not know how to solve it, or prepare for it, or escape it, and we do not know whether to escape it or seek it would be best. As a profound and penetrating thinker puts it: 'Neither the wicked nor the righteous finds satisfaction upon earth. Everything slips away from us, both the possession of what we desire and the enjoyment of what we possess. Every enjoyment means a loss, either for the body or the soul; and our existence dissolves in a succession of restless emotions, which destroy each other, and sweep us away in the stream of their engulfing nonentity.'[8]

And then there comes religion, and souls worn out with the wickedness and the weariness of this world, sick of their own failures and frailty, and torn with the sense of sin, throw wide the doors to a divine revelation of comfort and relief. I wonder how far the tumult, the passion, the power of what used to be called conversion is known to-day. No doubt it follows to some extent in the train of the sensational salvationists, but as one looks at the world about one, it seems as if the emotional experience of conversion must be rare and insignificant compared with the turbulent upheavals and spiritual renovations of the past.

Conversion is most typically familiar to us in connection with Christianity, but Professor Underwood, in his careful study of the subject, has shown that similar phenomena obtain with almost equal violence in the religions of the East and even in Mohammedanism. In Christian experience, at any rate, the sudden, prostrating realization of sin,

the overwhelming sense of the necessity of a new
life and of the possibility of entering into it, have
been prominent features from the beginning, and
on the very threshold we have the conversion of
Saint Paul, as one of the most dramatic elements in
forming the worship of Christ. Saint Augustine's
extraordinary renovation is almost equally celebrated, his long battle with selfishness and the en-
croaching passions of the world, and the final touch
of external emotional experience which forever
lifted him out of himself, and gave him a hold upon
the new life that he had been seeking. It does not
necessarily follow that the fundamental outlines
of character are altered by the conversional experience. Qualities that were always latent may
simply become active. Qualities that were always
patent may be given a new force or working. But
at least the effect is one of great modification, if
not of total change.

The psychological analysis of the process of conversion, as given by James and Starbuck, seems to
involve a sense of conflict in the soul, of divided
issues, of divided personality, as James expresses
it, at any rate of the tyrannous, insistent lower I
striving to assert itself against more spiritual in-
fluences, with an utter exhaustion of effort and a

burden of intolerable despair. The agony of inadequacy, of failure, of sin which one understands but cannot shake off, shatters and wrenches the crushed spirit with unspeakable mental and sometimes physical distress. The moderate church-goer of the present day would hardly understand the horror of one picture presented by the revivalist Finney: 'Accustomed as I was to seeing persons under great conviction, I must confess that his appearance gave me a tremendous shock. He was writhing in agony, grinding his teeth, and literally gnawing his tongue for pain. He cried out to me, "O Mr. Finney! I am lost! I am a lost soul!" I was greatly shocked and exclaimed, "If this is conviction, what is hell?"' [9] Cases like this are recorded over and over again, with endless suggestion of others unrecorded. And it was not only a question of individuals, but in the great revival movements, whole multitudes were carried away at once by similar upheavals of remorse and terror.

Then there came the presence of God, the exquisite touch of Christ upon the heart, the assurance of his salvation, bringing into it comfort and hope, and the relief and ecstasy were apparently as poignant as the despair had been. For the moment, at any rate, sin and the burden of sin were cast

behind, and the radiance of pure joy filled and overwhelmed the spirit with a rapture of delight. It is
true that from this point of view salvation was
largely negative. This is clear as to salvation
through Buddha: '"Even as the ocean has everywhere but one taste — that of salt — so my doctrine
has everywhere but one essence — that of deliverance," said Gautama!' [10] And Professor Starbuck
points out that conversion is 'a process of struggle
away from sin rather than of striving toward right-
eousness.' [11] But where the escape is so immense,
the mere appreciation of it carries positive delight in
itself. With the assurance of conversion, with the
confidence of a life renewed, there came a fresh splendor in the simplest functions of existence, a larger
glory with even the inanimate manifestations of the
external world. As Jonathan Edwards expressed
it, of himself: 'God's excellency, his wisdom, his
purity and love, seemed to appear in everything; in
the sun, moon, and stars; in the clouds and blue
sky; in the grass, flowers, and trees; in the water
and all nature; which used greatly to fix my mind.' [12]
Life is made over, men are made over, hope is made
over, and large realms of rapturous accomplishment open themselves in never ending vistas of
security and peace. As an enthusiastic sympathizer

of Moody puts it: 'He exulted in the free grace of God. . . . His joy was contagious. Men leaped out of darkness into light and lived a Christian life afterwards.' [13]

III

It is just in this afterwards that the main interest of conversion comes. It is easy enough to work on men's emotions with a momentary repentance and a momentary resolve. But does it last? Professor Underwood, in his dispassionate, psychological study, insists that it does. 'The most remarkable fruit of conversion is seen in the manner in which it has brought about complete and permanent deliverance from every known sin. Indisputable evidence on this point is so abundant that we are embarrassed with a wealth of riches.' [14]

If this is true, conversion was indeed a magnificent spiritual instrument, and the loss of it would be a deplorable deprivation for humanity. For the force of sin, of the intruding, persistent, encroaching I, consists precisely in its obstinate, everlasting reiteration. You think you have conquered forever, that the new life is securely established. Then the old habits reappear, the subtle temptations insinuate, and suddenly, before you know it, all is lost. There are indeed sane, simple natures, which sustain themselves instinctively in wholesome balance, and are not concerned about these convulsions at all. As Madame de Sévigné has it: 'I observe that there are souls, as straight as lines, loving virtue as naturally as horses trot.' [15] And again, there are those who can avoid soul-sickness, can avert disorder and spiritual malady, by mere common-sense, by that richest and rarest of gifts, a calm and sure control of their own thoughts and mental kingdom. As Landor says: 'It is as much at your arbitration on what theme you shall meditate, as in what meadow you shall botanize, and you have as much at your option the choice of your thoughts, as of the keys in your harpsichord.' [16] But for many, if not for most, this agency of calm control is wofully inadequate, and the thick onset of temptation is difficult to deal with without other aid than our own mere intelligence supplies.

There are the temptations of sex, which we do not speak of in good society, but which beset and torment with varied irritation both high and low and wise and unwise. Sometimes it is the mere incessant vexation of physical susceptibility or need, sometimes there is the even more overwhelming spur of sentimental passion, by which the engrossing charm of one particular object seems to subdue and dissipate all the claims of moral restraint.

Or it is the plague of money. Perhaps comparatively few feel the temptation of great crimes. To most of us, with staid habits and training, the risk, independent of moral considerations, seems always more than any possible advantage. But there are the thousand little hazy forms of half dishonesty, the disregard of an obligation, the disputing of a bill, the adjustment of a doubtful claim, misrepresentation of one's duty in taxes, or in customs returns. Who has not felt the temptation in some of these? Who has not yielded to it, in one shape or another, and looked upon himself afterwards with an infinite disgust?

And there is the disguise of temptation in apparently harmless pleasure. The severe moralists protest against dancing, or did when there were such things as severe moralists. No doubt there are persons to whom dancing is no more than a charming physical, rhythmical exercise. But there are thousands of others to whom it is a more or less direct sexual excitation, especially in these days when the quality of the dance and the dress, or undress, of the dancers, are all designed to effect this excitation in the highest degree. So with the theatre, and indeed with all the arts, which from their very nature are exquisitely intertwined with sin. But the theatre, by its light, its color, its atmosphere and the intensely human flavor connected with it, seems above all to accentuate the sensual preoccupations of the I and to dissipate restraint in poignant impulses of passionate intensity. It is no mere vulgar revivalist, but the highly trained and scholarly saintliness of a Pascal, which protests against the theatre as follows: 'All the great forms of entertainment are dangerous for Christian life; but among all those that the world has invented none is more to be feared than the theatre. It is a representation of the passions so delicate and natural, that it arouses them and gives birth to them in our hearts, and above all to that of love: especially when it is represented as chaste and above reproach.' [17]

The form of sin and temptation that most lends itself to the efforts of those who describe such things is the thirst for stimulants or drugs, since this is not unduly indecorous in the description and is attended with such disastrously lurid results. But the details of temptation here are the same as in other forms, the persistently recurring desire, the battle fought for a time perhaps with courage, then the gradual succumbing of an infinite weariness.

There is the pestilently intruding suggestion of the enemy at all times and in all places. Worst of all, one takes part, as it were, against oneself. One finds the best of excuses for yielding, and the worst of reasons for carrying on the fight. As one who had waged a long and finally a successful war against alcohol puts it: 'I would frame many excuses for myself — plead my own cause before myself, as judge and jury, until I obtained at my own hands a willing acquittal.' [18] Then comes the defeat, and the shame, and the infinite disgust, and the old, weary battle has to be begun over again. If these more melodramatic struggles seem far away from some of us, do we not all know the same thing in some form, the struggle with temper, the struggle with indolence, the struggle with selfishness, the ever-renewed struggle with the besetting, persistent, voracious, unconquerable I?

And then comes in the power of Christ, the acquisition of an ally who seems to bring with him a dominating force beside which the mere unaided efforts of the human will are insignificant. 'There is only one way to teach virtue, to teach religion,' said Joubert,[19] and Joubert was by no means a fanatic, though to the present day such a saying may seem fantastic and unnecessary. What this added power, which comes through Christ and the acceptance of salvation through him, may be or may mean, is another question. You may explain it psychologically however you please. There can be no question as to the fact. Men who have been hopelessly possessed by the devil of drink, have accepted Christ, and have flung drink behind them forever. Men who have found the sexual burden as impossible to throw off as it was intolerable to bear, have gone to Christ for help, have filled their lives with Christ, and then have looked back with wonder and pity at their former slavery. How the change is wrought, who of us can say, or rather, there are many ways of saying. That it is wrought is incontrovertible, indisputable.

And this involving, controlling love and 'power of Christ can even achieve its last and fundamental victory in the overcoming and casting out of the fundamental human weakness, fear. The supreme triumph of faith and hope would seem to be in the sacrifice of the martyrs, who walked through fire with joy and serenity in the love of their Lord. They had their flesh beaten and torn and wrenched and bruised and scorched and mangled, and they bore it in ecstatic contemplation of what Christ had done for them, and would do.

This, I confess, passes my comprehension. Physical pain is such a horror to me that I cannot conceive how I could endure torture rather than give up any faith. I read in the Journal of Eugénie de Guérin: 'This water that scalds me a little makes me think of the martyrs, of the baths of melted lead and oil and boiling water, in which they were plunged. . . . What should I have done in the place of Blandina? God knows that I should probably have done as she did, for faith renders us superhuman, and I believe I have faith.' [20] I have no faith and cannot conceive having any that would enable me to endure such things. Yet I suppose my flesh and blood are like the flesh and blood of those who did endure them.

The supreme instrument in all this struggle and victory is prayer, turning to God, through Christ or otherwise, and so adding the force of the eternal to the petty human power of resistance and combat. The efficacy of prayer in accomplishing merely external, material objects may be denied. You may or may not believe that the course of nature will be modified at the request of a believing heart. But as to the psychological value of prayer, its availing power in helping to banish sin, to resist temptation, to sweep away spiritual coldness and hardness and

indifference, there can be no question whatever.
You may explain these effects by divine interposition, or by mere psychological action, but they are
there. When the storms of evil beset you, when the
thickest blasts of desire overwhelm, if you can turn
to Christ, and earnestly, passionately become absorbed in the thought of his help, it will not fail you.
I myself, who have lost all hold upon prayer and
have not resorted to it for years, yet know from my
own experience what a mighty and prevailing refuge it can be. The whole of human history is full of
records of a similar nature, and instances could be
produced everywhere. But one that has peculiarly
touched me lately is the account of Samuel Pepys,
the hardened man of the world, sceptical, indifferent, in the ordinary course of life, yet when a special
wave of disaster overcomes him in the form of
sexual temptation and its consequences, throwing
himself upon his knees in ardent entreaty, and all
the while mixing daily common affairs with his
spiritual appeal: 'Did this night begin to pray to
God upon my knees alone in my chamber, which
God knows I cannot yet do heartily; but I hope God
will give me the grace more and more every day to
fear Him, and to be true to my poor wife. This
night the upholsterers did finish hanging of my best

chamber, but my sorrow and trouble is so great about this business, that it puts me out of all joy in looking upon it or minding how it was.' [21]

IV

So far we have been occupied with the resistance to sin and temptation by ordinary human beings, by you and me, in the daily current of life. But there are also the saints, who make such resistance as it were a profession, and a great part of whose business is the denial of human needs and desires. That is to say, what in us is a necessity, and usually a grudging one, becomes in them a delight. They deny themselves not only on their own account, but above all that they may afford an effective example to others; and so practised and developed, the habit of denial may grow to be in itself a source of endless satisfaction and even joy.

The first secret of this denial is to show that life may be simple. 'Life should be simple, gentle, and sincere: what is there more?' We have gathered about our ordinary lives, especially in these modern days of elaborate material equipment, an immense accumulation of luxurious habit, which has become so thoroughly habit that it ceases even to afford us pleasure or satisfaction; yet we are restless and dis-

contented at the thought of its being taken away.
The first effort of the saint in all ages has been to
show and prove that all this material involvement
of comfort and luxury is perfectly dispensable, that
it not only does not help but hinders the freedom
and energy of the spiritual life. The saint eschews
elegance of clothing, delicacy of food, ease of repose, grace and ornament of social intercourse, not
because these things are harmful in themselves, but
because they distract from higher, purer, inner interests and objects, which well and consistently
followed, more than console for any material loss.

And in getting rid of these minor needs, the saints
have always struck straight at the root of all
evil, the love, the possession, the accumulation of
money. Jesus would have none of it, for himself
and his disciples, and though the followers of Jesus
have struggled desperately to reconcile God and
Mammon, those who have truly felt his influence
have again and again striven to return to the simple
principle of his law. And we have Saint Francis,
worshipping lovely poverty, insisting that she is the
secret and the foundation of the higher life. And
centuries later we have Wesley declaring passionately to his clergy a gospel almost like that of
Francis: 'I will take care (God being my helper)

that none of the accursed thing shall be found in my tents, when the Lord calleth me hence. . . . If I leave behind me £10 above my debts and my books, or what may be due on account of them — you and all mankind bear witness against me that I lived and died a thief and a robber.' [22]

Not so very many years ago, right here in America, there were a boy and a girl who were about to be married. They had comfortable means, but they had become possessed with ideas like those of Christ and Saint Francis as to simple living, casting aside dress and elegance and luxury, building a small peasant's house, contenting themselves with the plainest satisfaction of daily needs, giving away their superfluity, and finding their solace and their joy in the higher things of the spirit. Their elders mocked at them and scolded them, and finally persuaded or compelled them to put the ideal aside and settle back to the old, conventional, fleshly routine, so far, far from what Jesus and Saint Francis taught. I wonder if they would be happier now, if they had not given way.

As the saints deny and subdue material needs, so they endeavor to practise the denial of the passions in every form. Chastity was as essential to Saint Francis as poverty, and the two went together and helped each other. There are temperance and control in all their aspects. Lust is overcome, greed is overcome, wrath is overcome, envy is overcome. And what here again makes the peculiar character-istic of saintliness is the joy in doing all these things. It is not that denial is a burden, or an effort, or a misery: it becomes a habit of delight, through constant contemplation of the higher ends to be attained.

Further, there is the denial of the will, that cen-tre and stronghold of the tyrannous, persistent I. There is the lesson of humility. Everywhere the I has its obstinate, aggressive inclination to insist upon its own excellence, its own superiority, even when this is mainly done to overcome an inner con-sciousness of the opposite. The first, constant, im-possible task of the saints is to root this out, not only to manifest, but to feel, that one is inferior to others. Heaven knows there is always ground for such feeling, but the I shuns it, avoids it, hates it, is determined to emphasize the points of superiority and let the others go. And the saints bend all their effort to form the habit of humility in them-selves and to teach it to those who look to them for help and guidance. 'It is not enough to detach one-self,' says Fénelon; 'one should belittle oneself.

By detachment one renounces external things; by belittling one renounces oneself. We should recognize our littleness in everything, and count what one has worth nothing, one's virtue and one's courage least of all.' [23] And the 'Imitation' has it more perfectly and simply still: 'It does you no harm to put yourself below all others; it harms you infinitely to prefer yourself to even one.' [24]

As the inward subjection of the will comes in humility, so the outward shows itself in complete obedience. Here again the I resists desperately. It may on a pinch yield to persuasion, it may combine and compromise for common ends. To obey absolutely, to put aside one's own judgment, to submit to the will of another, not because it is better or wiser, but simply for the principle of obedience, this is a hard task to learn. The soldier learns it in practice; but within he may nourish what rebellious spirit he pleases. The saint strives to make the obedience spiritual as well as temporal, to resign not only his conduct but his heart, into the hands of his superiors and to God acting through them, that so the ends of God in the world may be utterly accomplished. 'Obedience is never pure and tranquil,' says Montaigne, 'in him who reasons and argues.' [25] The sacrifice must be final and complete. William James, writing in the true spirit of the twentieth century, finds such a sacrifice hard to understand: 'It is difficult even imaginatively to comprehend how men possessed of an inner life of their own could ever have come to think the subjection of its will to that of other finite creatures recommendable. I confess that to myself it seems something of a mystery.' [26] But it must be remembered that it was always the will of God working through the finite creatures, and for my part, if one was convinced that it was the will of God, such absolute subjection seems to me a means not only of enormous power but of enormous comfort.

Finally, as the aim must be to deny and overcome the I, so there must always be the effort to express that denial in external details of privation or even suffering. Vestiges of this denial still linger in the un-self-denying twentieth century with those faithful persons who, during Lent, endeavor to give up some little indulgence, harmless in itself, but regretted, and therefore valuable in its loss for purposes of discipline. When you habitually smoke two cigars a day, to cut down to one or even none for six weeks, represents the overcoming of the I to a certain extent. And those, like myself, who have never in a long life sacrificed a single thing for the sake of discipline, can but look on and wonder. But the sacrifice, the discipline, the humiliation of the I, with the older saints, went much farther than the abandonment of cigars. The body must be brutalized, must learn that comfort was of no consequence compared to doing the will of God. Even health must be sacrificed. Hear Saint Teresa on the subject: 'Be convinced, sisters, that you came here to die for Christ, not to indulge yourselves for Him. The devil suggests that we need to take care of ourselves in order to observe the Rule. Such nuns are so exceedingly anxious to preserve their health so that they may be able to obey the Rule that they die without ever having observed it for a month, or perhaps, even for a single day. If good health is our object in life, I do not know why we came here.' [27]

And the maltreatment of the body went so far as self-inflicted torture, hair-shirts worn next the skin, violent, cruel, bloody scourgings, flagellations. The subtle, morbid analysis of Freudian and general modern psychology seeks to trace curious freaks of sex in all these efforts. No doubt such freaks existed and do still. But to me the self-tormenting seems more naturally the outcome of the bitter, direct warfare upon the I. In any case, there have been ages when such things reached the

point of epidemic mania. This is Gebhart's picture
of them: 'In 1260, the great Joachimite year, the
flagellants appeared in northern Italy. "All, high
and low, nobles, soldiers, the common people, naked
to the waist, marched in procession through the
cities and lashed and scourged themselves, preceded
by the bishops and the clergy."' [28] Such an experience seems inconceivable enough in an American
city of to-day. We smile at what we call the folly,
the absurdity, the morbid extravagance of it. What
good could it do to God or man? Yet I can perfectly well imagine a tornado of the spirit sweeping
even American self-complacence into similar out-
breaks. There are times when we find the I a damn-
able thing. No symbol of the conquest of it is too
violent, or too extravagant. And he ill or little understands the human heart who is not able to enter
into the beauty and the grandeur of asceticism even
in its most arduous forms.

V

But this coldness, this ridicule, this indifference
of the world, in all times, drove the saints to shun it
and escape it, and to seek remote solitudes, where
they could follow out their ideal in sequestered
peace. *Monasticism* means, etymologically, the cult

of solitude, and solitude with their own souls had for the saints an indescribable, seductive charm. There are always souls for whom it has a charm, even in the twentieth century, which seems to offer less inducements to solitude, and less room for it. Doubtless the ideal would be a life in which solitude and society were wisely mixed. But humanity rarely runs to wise mixtures. One habit or the other proves engrossing, enthralling. If you have the habit of going, you go, from sheer hatred of staying still. If you have the habit of seeing human faces, you cannot live without them. On the other hand, the habit of silence and quiet grows in attractiveness, the more you cultivate it. There is no more exquisite sentence in the 'Imitation' than the untranslatable, simple one: 'Cella continuata dulcescit, et male custodita tædium generat.' [29] Learn to live with your own soul, and you will find it, if not always delightful company, at least more soothing than the other souls which you are always seeking and never find at all.

Of course solitude in all shapes has its dangers. The fantastic vagaries of hermits and recluses, even with a religious preoccupation, brought spiritual disorder and sometimes madness with them. But the ideal is one so far removed from the habits of to-day that the sympathetic contemplation of it cannot do us very serious harm and may be of a good deal of benefit. And all the value of such isolated effort toward the pure rapture of the divine is summed up once more in two perfect words of the 'Imitation': 'fruitive quiescere.' [30] So many of us keep a vast stir with no profit at all!

As the limitations of humanity with regard to isolation and solitude became irresistibly evident, there developed the tendency to seek escape from the world and to cultivate the religious life by binding together men and women in communities. For a thousand years the monasteries and nunneries exercised an enormous influence, for good and evil both, and even to-day the influence is by no means extinct. In the darker and more violent periods of history such institutions served as an admirable refuge for quiet or infirm spirits, who were disinclined or unequal to fighting their way in harsh and militant surroundings. And there is no question but that those who were disposed to the inner life found rich and varied encouragement for it in the means that the church offered them for developing and satisfying their longing for God and for spiritual things. The peace, the infinite solace, the elevation above all earthly needs and cares, that breathe through the pages of the 'Imitation,' may have been beyond the reach of many, perhaps of most, but there were always some who profited by them. And the habit of inward concentration was of benefit to those who did not and could not carry it to the highest limits of ecstasy. A lady who had been educated in a convent told me the other day that, even though she had become indifferent to Catholic belief, the practice of contemplation, the power of throwing aside daily cares and turning her whole soul within, was an immense relief and comfort, and she wondered how her Protestant friends could live without it.

Also, the monasteries meant far more than idle solitude. They meant work, hard work, useful work, and what they did for education, for the care of the poor, and for the general encouragement of industry, in times when the world had little thought for such things, is altogether inestimable.

No doubt the life had its defects, which are obvious enough. Many were seduced into it, or forced into it, who were entirely unfitted for it, and the result was often discontent, irritation, and the fostering of all sorts of evils and vices, which may have been exaggerated, but which are proved to have existed by abundant and irrefragable testimony.

226

Yet, as with the excesses of asceticism, no one can understand the full depth or the full beauty of human nature who does not enter into the charm and the grandeur of the monastic ideal. I have never visited the Grande Chartreuse, which seems to embody that ideal most fully, and which, alas, the French Government has now secularized, obliterating at a stroke the accumulated dignity and sanctity of ages. But in the exquisite Certosa at Florence, with its peaceful, sequestered cloisters, on their high hilltop, under the Tuscan sky, I have dreamed of the infinite peace, or the near approach to heaven, that one might enjoy there, cultivating one's little garden and one's little soul, if one only believed. No one who shares this feeling can fail to appreciate the significance of Matthew Arnold's poem, which has the Grande Chartreuse for its title, and which expresses the passionate regret that comes to one who has lost belief, yet longs for all these things that belief might carry with it. And the poem ends with the reply of the recluses to those who would rally them out of their ancient faith:

> Long since we pace this shadowed nave;
> We watch those yellow tapers shine,
> Emblems of hope over the grave,
> In the high altar's depth divine.
> The organ carries to our ear
> Its accents of another sphere.

LIFE AND I

Fenced early in this cloistral round
Of revery, of shade, of prayer,
How should we grow in other ground?
How can we flower in foreign air?
— Pass, banners, pass, and bugles, cease;
And leave our desert to its peace.

VI

But we are studying the omnipresent I, and it is easy enough to trace it even in the self-denial of the saints. The busy, impertinent, insolent I resents control of any kind, and repression, unnatural, violent repression, only forces it to break out with corresponding violence at some other point. The Freudians have made a philosophy out of this business of repression, and have traced the I's pugnacity and fury of resistance, with all the strange abortions of thwarted conflict, even in our dreams, in fact have made our dreams nothing but the dimly woven tissue of it. And the wisdom and the value of the Freudian study have shown in the increasing tendency rather to divert, to guide, and to develop energy in useful, healthy directions, than to allow it to expend itself in the mad effort to subdue and overcome.

But, with or without a philosophy to support it, humanity has always made passionate protest against the effort to force it too long and too

severely into the ways of artificial virtue. Individuals, in all ages, have rebelled, and thrown off
the yoke utterly. They said, 'After all, your laws
are yours only, concocted by human ingenuity, too
often for human purposes: why should I tear myself
to pieces to submit to them?' And in rejecting what
was evil and excessive, they have gone to the other
extreme, and recognized no law and no wise guidance except the immediate whim and passion of the
moment. These sharp and violent outbursts of reaction have affected not only individuals here and
there, they have affected whole communities and
epochs. Thus, it is impossible not to see in the
sensual excesses of the Restoration period in England the direct revolt against the too severe repression of the Puritan government of the Common-
wealth. So in early New England. The narrow
habit, the too harsh unworldliness, of the first
generations, blighted and withered the emotional
side of humanity, till it was forced to find some outlet somewhere, and as the only outlet it could then
conceive was religious, its religion took on the extravagant features of the eighteenth-century revival. An English observer of these revivals asked
an American friend, why, with so much restraint
in society, in business, in education, and in politics,

'do you have these great excitements in religion? How is it that you who do everything else by *calculation*, trust this to passion?' [31] The answer of the American friend is not recorded, but it should obviously have been that the outbreak came just because the repression in all other aspects was so severe.

As the I rebels in direct revolt, so even more it protests and escapes restraint by hypocrisy, by comfortably pretending an outward acquiescence with all the denial that is demanded of it, and at the same time secretly indulging its natural inclination in decorous licentiousness. It should be insisted that there are probably far fewer elaborate, conscious hypocrites than is commonly supposed. We are all of us ready to attribute to others motives which we should not tolerate in ourselves. No doubt there have been and are persons who systematically feign virtue to achieve their purposes. But human nature so easily and skilfully deceives itself, that it is wiser to assume in most cases a reconciliation of nominally virtuous aim with selfish practice.

Yet we all of us know, or should know, how largely hypocrisy enters into our lives, the little minor pretences, without which the world could hardly go on. If we all at all times bared completely our thoughts of our neighbors and our thoughts of ourselves and in ourselves, the social compromise could not be sustained for a moment. Yet it is no doubt true that artificial, or extreme, repression does much aggravate the hypocritical tendency, and the I even in the saints is rarely so much crushed as it appears to be.

It shows itself curiously even in direct, deliberate, and apparently successful denial. Thus, a strange, perverted form of the desire to excel is the desire to excel in sin, in order to emphasize repentance, and those who cannot surpass their fellows in well doing, sometimes display a surprising ingenuity in making themselves our superiors in wickedness. This often appears in a certain class of confessions and autobiographies. The 'Confessions' of Rousseau are notable for it, and I feel always an artificial quality in the 'Confessions' of Augustine, through the Saint's obvious desire to stress the wicked inclinations of his heart, when perhaps he was never so very bad, after all.

Again, the subtle habit of excelling and of taking comfort in it, seems to intrude into even the very methods and practices that are adopted to subdue it. You overcome your dearest inclinations and temptations — and are proud of it. You deprive

yourself, discipline yourself, torment yourself —
and are proud of it. As La Mère Angélique de
Saint Jean complained: 'My soul was not sufficiently humiliated, for I thought only of the glory
there was in suffering for the truth.' [32] Even in
humility, even in those who cultivate the vastest
readiness to subordinate themselves to others, to
help others, to live for others, still lingers the accursed tendency to exalt oneself because of one's
humiliation, the deep reluctance to accept, though
one is always so ready to give and gain the gratifi-
cation of giving. And Fénelon murmurs with a
sigh: 'I should like to oblige all the human race,
especially the good; but there is hardly a person to
whom I should be willing to be obliged.' [33] If this is
not pride, what is? So in the last extreme of denial,
perfect and unreasoning obedience, the saints themselves have detected the lingering vestiges of self-
satisfaction. For if one obeys more quickly, more
perfectly, more efficiently, than others, one is usually aware of it, and finds a certain smug comfort in
the awareness. And the very habit of obedience,
the teaching of it, the preaching of it, the eminent
practicing of it, are quite compatible with a terrible and enduring pride. As Mr. Sedgwick says of
Loyola, whose cardinal rule for himself, and for his

order, was obedience, 'At bottom he was a very proud man; and after his death his pride seems to have infected the whole order.' [34] Thus it is clear that that persistent, subtle, inevitable I is not so easily subdued, even by those who make the highest, the noblest, the most unfailing endeavor.

VII

But in this prolonged, unceasing, perhaps hopeless battle with the I, it will hardly be denied that Christ, the belief in Christ, the acceptance of Christ, has been one of the most mighty and effective instruments. For centuries those who have been driven almost to despair by the persistent onset of their sins and passions, and the warring tumult in their members, have turned to that high, pure source of strength and comfort, and found peace. Will this be so any more, or in any such degree? To me it appears that the chief value of this agency of Christ lies in the belief in his divinity, his actual oneness with God, and as a consequence of that oneness, his taking upon himself the sins of humanity and by his divine mediation washing them away. Does the world longer believe in that divinity? Will it believe in it again? No doubt many millions still do, or say they do. But even with them, does the belief take hold and work with the mighty and irresistible force which pertained to it in older times? And if it is gone, can it ever come back? Can it be that in this great material America of ours, with its mad luxury, its constant necessities of indulgence and bodily comfort, its overwhelming external hurry and tumult of distraction, there should come again a surging tide of Christian belief, and sweep the world into the ideal conceptions that it had a thousand years ago? It seems impossible, yet who can say? And meantime the riot of the I is as gorgeous, as tumultuous, as unchecked, as self-exultant as it has ever been.

CHAPTER VII
CHRIST AND MORE THAN I
I

THE effort to overcome and to escape the I by direct conquest and subdual has been seen to have its drawbacks and to be not altogether satisfactory. A far more effective method is to seek to lose the I, to forget it, to merge it, in the life of others. We have found a striking illustration of this in the desperate, foiled attempt to seek spiritual union through sexual love. Again, in ordinary social intercourse the I endeavors to escape its inner preoccupations by using others in direct diversion and amusement. But it is a far more serious matter to make the positive effort to increase the joy of others, or even more to relieve or to diminish their sorrow.

And it will be seen at once that the world offers an illimitable field for activity of this sort. The most convinced, indomitable optimist will hardly deny the reality or the immensity of human suffering, and the instant it is admitted, the relief of it becomes one of the highest of human purposes, even if it is to be relieved partly by the argument that it does not exist. It is curious to reflect upon the growth and development of the habit of general pity. A profound sense of it is of course evident in the teaching of Jesus, and the keenest appreciation of universal sorrow and misery seems to be largely at the bottom of the religion of Buddha: 'Now by the roadside, as he beheld the ploughmen, plodding along the furrows, and the writhing worms, his heart again was moved with piteous feeling, and anguish pierced his soul afresh.' [1] But in the bustling, external western world the passion of pity grew more slowly. Renan points out that it was for lack of pity that the old Roman society came to destruction.[2] And only by degrees did the imaginative feeling of the universal misery of sentient life come to its climax of intensity in the nineteenth century. Such a remark as that of Keats, 'Health and spirits can only belong unalloyed to the selfish man — the man who thinks much of his fellows can never be in spirits,' [3] would have been hardly comprehensible to a Greek, or to a Florentine of the Renaissance. Within the last hundred years this passion of pity has extended itself to animals in a way never conceived before, and over-sensitive hearts derive, as did Buddha, acute agony from the writhing of a worm. It is even possible that the huge increase of this imaginative power of pity has on the whole increased the sum of suffering, instead of diminishing it, in spite of the resultant philanthropic effort. Especially in the case of many persons, who have largely lost any belief in the future life as a world of compensation, this sense of misery has become so haunting that it sours and darkens any possibility of individual enjoyment. The huge epic of Zola is significant not only in its sordid ugliness, but because it above all embodies and vivifies this spectacle of universal suffering, and so deserves to be called in the deepest sense, the epic of pity. And Nietzsche's vigorous doctrine of the Superman emphasizes a protest against pity in its corrupt and debilitating excess.

But undoubtedly the true course is not to dwell upon the suffering as a mere matter of the imagination, but to make every possible effort to diminish the total of it, even a little, and to increase as far as possible the sum of joy. And thus we get the instinctive idealist, the man or woman whose life lies in the struggle to make over humanity, to make men worthy of a happier lot, and to see that they get it. As Shelley said, with his intense felicity: 'I was born with a passion for reforming the world.' Tempers like Montaigne, like Goethe, who are born with an immense curiosity, or an immense capacity for enjoyment, can look only with wonder and sometimes with contempt, upon these bustling spirits who are never satisfied to let good and evil rest as they are. We all of us get impatient with the idealists, and sometimes wish them different, but most of us have a corner in our being that sympathizes with them and at least envies the intense delight they find in their struggle itself.

Their general defects are obvious enough. They are sometimes persistent, one-sided, dogmatic, to the point of cruelty. Those who do not like their methods must get out of the way, or be crushed, if it is possible to crush them. Then a too high ideal always carries its penalties with it. If it is your business in life to fight evil, to get rid of evil, if this combat is the chief thing that makes you feel alive, you are naturally inclined to magnify evil somewhat for your own purposes, even to imagine it where it does not exist. The world has its good points, and those of us who are not too particular manage to stumble along with it as it is, without any violent effort to improve it. But the born idealist is not content with any such tolerance as this. Every bit of evil must be eliminated, and to be eliminated it must be traced to its murkiest hiding-places, where a more moderate spirit might be disposed to let it linger.

Another curious feature of idealism is the perversion by which it so readily turns to a pessimistic view. If your ideal is too high, if you are constantly trying the world by a too exalted standard, the mere mediocrity of life exasperates, and you cry out against things that are in themselves indifferent and sometimes even amusing. The humorous attitude is of all attitudes the one with which the idealist feels least at home. After all, to love men, as well as to laugh at them, it is perhaps desirable not to start by thinking too well of them; otherwise one is apt to be disappointed. As a keen observer has it: 'We should never imagine that men are too good, for fear of finding out later that they are too bad.' [4] The great pessimists of the world are all born idealists and Leopardi's passionate despair of humanity comes from expecting far too much of it. For all which, or because of all which, it must always be insisted that idealism, and even sometimes pessimism, contains the true nobility of the world.

II

The idealists, those who have a passion for reform, may work from the point of view of this life, or from that of another. And of course the two attitudes are often intermingled, yet perhaps not so often as might be imagined. Those who have a profound conviction of eternity are sometimes indifferent to the concerns of this dusty earth and neglectful of them, and the most passionate effort and activity to make over life here are apt to come from those who do not trouble themselves about life hereafter.

There are the political reformers. Ever since men began to gather into organized communities, for protection and progress, thinkers and reasoners have speculated on the means of governing those communities and have devised schemes by which such government might be bettered from the bungling, makeshift, hand-to-mouth procedure which it too often is. Aristocracy, monarchy, and democracy, empire and republic, much government and no government at all, each has found its advocate, and the most extravagant theory has often had supporters ready to fight and die for it. Meantime, the actual practice of government goes on much in its old, blundering, practical, daily way, and the interesting thing is that, for the most part, the governing is not in the hands of the theorists at all, who, if they do ever attempt it, make a mess of it, but is

rather carried on by hard-headed, limited oppor-
tunists, who see little further than the needs of the
hour and usually exemplify the admirable saying of
the prime minister of Bluebeard: 'It is by never
knowing whither I am tending myself that I have
succeeded in leading others.' [5]

As there are the political reformers, so there are
the philanthropists and social workers and theorists,
those who are passionately aware of human suffering, and of all the miseries, and especially of all the
unfair miseries, of life, and never weary in the
attempt to overcome or to get rid of them. Sometimes the passion shows in mere immediate helpfulness, in giving, and healing, and comforting, and
cheering, and there are plenty of noble souls, who
find their own highest satisfaction in yielding everything to such helpfulness, even their own health and
their own lives. Also, there are those whose attitude is more abstract, who are concerned less with
the practical relief of individuals, but think out and
seek to apply elaborate schemes of socialism, communism, and a dozen other isms, which afford vast
amusement to their contrivers, and sometimes even
seem to work indirectly to the general benefit.

Again, there are the moralists, who want to make
us better, by force, if necessary. And many persons

find these an offensive and vexatious generation. They are certainly often liable to two great criticisms: either they do not understand the vices and weaknesses they are trying to remedy, or they understand them too well. That is, they either endeavor to make over human nature, without fully entering into its strength or its limitations, or they lay themselves open to the suspicion of hypocrisy, by indulging, perhaps unconsciously, the very vices which they so bitterly attack. In any case, they are too apt to think that talk and external regulation can effect the deeper spiritual changes, which can be brought about only by some form of spiritual grace. Yet, for all the defects, their effort and their energy are often magnificent, and sometimes not wholly unprofitable.

It is interesting to note a few of the more general characteristics that stand out in connection with the reformers of this world. In the first place, it is undeniable that to one who merely looks on and criticises, their action is apt to appear unreasonable and even stupid. But it should be tolerantly remembered that this is because they act. Action, especially abstract and on the larger scale, is always laying itself open to these charges of stupidity, but it is so easy to judge it afterwards and so difficult before. The cold, the careful, the considerate, confine their action to what is strictly necessary, so as to be sure of safety at any rate. It is the eager, the impulsive, the generous, who, seeing the great end, refuse to debate the means too long, plunge in and take a chance, even if they know that some evil may happen along with the good.

Again, the reformer has, and too often deserves, the reputation of being unpractical. He will not make the concessions and compromises that the ordinary man of business knows must be made, if practical success is to be achieved. The reformer sees his goal brilliantly clear before him. He wants to go right at it direct, not to work back and forth through sinuous by-paths, through all sorts of hampering and trammelling bargains with iniquity, which in the end may drag him down instead of helping others up. And there is no doubt but that his goal is often not only far away, but altogether out of human reach, wild, extravagant, utopian, and that by setting it so high he induces mere discouragement and despair among the feebler and less earnest of his followers.

It is curious to note how frequently the passion for rebellion, for destruction, is mixed up with the eager longing to make the world over. The one thing that all reformers start with, no doubt justly enough, is the assumption that the world is vilely bad. If that is so, is not the first step, to get rid of these hateful, ugly institutions that exist? So long as they do exist and flourish, nothing whatever can be seriously done for betterment. Thus it happens that all great reforms carry in their train a large band of those who are merely born, natural, joyous rebels, who have no objection to something better, but who above all want something different, and are wildly eager to tear down, with comparatively little regard to who is to do the building up. Now there is enough that is evil in human institutions, and we all know it; but humanity has been a million years in developing them, with the best effort it was capable of, and perhaps the blind effort to destroy does not carry all gain with it.

It is extremely interesting to see how these instincts of destruction and belief blend together. As I look about me everywhere, I am convinced that the truest believer is not the conservative, but the earnest and passionate radical. He has such immense, magnificent confidence in his ideal, such enthusiastic trust in his own powers of achieving it, that he is ready and glad to lay his hand to destruction anywhere, secure that if he is to be the guide and master, better things must come afterward. On the other hand, the conservative is he who is profoundly sceptical, often to the point of utter nihilism. He mistrusts action, whether others' or his own. He sees just as clearly as the radical, often more clearly, the defects of what exists, but in his utter ignorance of means and ends for betterment, he says to himself, what is may be bad, but what might be would almost certainly be worse, and he hesitates to lift his foot for a single step into the dark, lest he should find nowhere to set it down. Hence, if radicalism means going to the roots of things, the nihilistic conservative of this type is the profoundest radical of all.

Thus the errors, the weaknesses, the defects, of the reformers are evident enough, and it is natural that the dispassionate observer should sometimes say with Montaigne, of all reforming efforts: 'We correct ourselves often quite as foolishly as we correct others.' [6] Yet who can resist the infectious passion of the born idealists? They sweep us away with them, even when they make us indignant, or more tragically make us mock, and the bitterest and most sceptical must needs admit that, for all the errors, it is the reforming spirit that makes the world go on.

LIFE AND I

III

Then there are the idealists of the other world, who may or may not care for the welfare of men here, but labor with profound and undying zeal to awaken them to a sense of the future and to prepare them for it. The tendency I have alluded to above, somewhat to exaggerate the evil of life on this earth, and the other tendency to prefer sinners and even to luxuriate in them, on the principle of Jesus, 'I came not to call the righteous, but sinners, to repentance,' [7] are perhaps unduly manifest in many reformers of this type. But no one can deny the force or the beauty of the passion for extending one's own belief and hope to others, for imparting to them the comfort and the ecstasy of one's own salvation. One sees this ardor in Saint Paul, at the very start. No sooner was his own life made over, no sooner had the faith and the hope of a new life through Christ taken possession of him, than he was overcome with the desire to disseminate this possession to all the world, and to make Jew and Gentile alike see and glory in the light and splendor of the Christian truth. And Paul has had his legion of successors in all sects everywhere. It was said of Buddha: 'Even as we desire to give peace to our children, so did he long to give rest to the world.' [8]

246

The true religious idealist, the true purveyor of the gospel, no sooner receives the light himself than he is seized with this passion for distributing it. As we see, for example in Moody, or in Booth, the instantaneous result of conversion is the impulse to convert others, to share as widely as possible the greatest joy and benefit that this world or any other has to give.

Perhaps the most impressive form of the religious idealistic zeal is that of the missionaries, those who leave home and friends and comfort to wander in strange lands and face hardship and misery for the sake of communicating the gospel message. It must be admitted at once that these messengers of hope are not free from some of the defects that beset the reforming class in general. Their knowledge and discretion are not always equal to their zeal, and being by their calling bound to action and perpetually busy with it, they lay themselves open to ill-natured and not wholly unjust criticism from those who would never have a tithe of their persistence or a tithe of their courage. Their energy is sometimes expended in the wrong place, and is sometimes pitiable, and sometimes even lends itself to mockery. Yet the splendor of their spirit and often the grandeur of their achievement should be recognized by even the most critical. The ardor appears in all faiths and in all sects, and the Buddhist or the Mohammedan is as ready to go every length in spreading his belief as the most earnest Christian. That some evils and some disadvantages are associated with missionary effort will hardly be denied, but the best testimony to what has been accomplished is that of men like Stevenson and Darwin, who in no way share the missionaries' faith, but have had intimate experience of all the good they do, and are perfectly ready to certify to it and to foster it. While for pure ideal self-sacrifice, for utter willingness to meet privation and even death and torture for their cause, the lofty effort of the missionaries has never been surpassed, and he who doubts it has only to read Parkman's vivid narratives of the doings and sufferings of the Jesuit apostles among the Indians, which again can be paralleled by many others less known but not less impressive. The magnificent courage and enthusiasm which lie at the bottom of the effort cannot be better indicated than in Mr. Sedgwick's sentence in regard to Loyola's personal crusade into the Holy Land: 'I cannot but feel . . . that he hoped to convert the Turks and win Jerusalem single-handed.' [9] Single-handed, but with the whole power of God behind!

Then, as well as the spreading of the Gospel abroad, there is the preaching of it at home. In an earlier chapter I have suggested the defects of the sermon. As we all know, it can be perhaps the vastest instrument of boredom, and in thousands of pulpits all over the United States to-day well meaning but infinitely dull and tedious persons are deluging too often vacancy with an amplitude of emptiness which is none the more tolerable for being expected and none the more effective for being ever renewed. If the Protestant Church is killed, it will be the sermon that has killed it. Yet it is the very power and splendor of the instrument that has caused it to be so misused and abused by those who are quite incapable of handling it. And the effects produced by great preachers in all ages have been so immense that one does not wonder that the Church is tempted to place upon preaching a far greater burden than it will bear.

It is not only the matter but the manner, not only the doctrine, but the man. Take the great French preachers of the seventeenth century, Bossuet, Massillon, Bordaloue. Their printed sermons to-day may have power and literary beauty. Still, few of us find them exciting reading. But turn to the pages of Madame de Sévigné, and hear her account of the tumult those men could stir in the hearts of some who listened to them. Take in our own day right here the sermons of Phillips Brooks. To read, they are no doubt excellent in their bearing and purpose, but still, as one reads, one wonders just what it was that moved people. Those who remember know what it was: the noble, impressive, animated figure, the voice which seemed to carry the heart in every tone of it, the swift, turbulent, passionate, overwhelming utterance, which aimed to leave no single soul in the vast congregation untouched, unsearched, unillumined, or unsaved.

And as these great preachers know how to think and to speak, so they instinctively understand their audiences, know how to deal with them, to think their thoughts, to live their lives, to seize the right moment and the right method for going straight to the heart. Every touch and turn of outward event or circumstance is utilized. Every possibility of spiritual suggestion is turned to account, not with deliberate cunning, though sometimes this may be suspected, but with a passionate instinct for carrying out the highest purpose in the most effective and permanent way. Take music, for instance. The great preacher knows well how mighty it is, knows what it can do to assist him. He picks the hymn that suits his subject, gets his people on fire with the tune or the words, so that their spiritual sensibilities are strained to the highest point of tension and responsiveness. Then he makes his own appeal, to carry on the movement of the music, and makes it, as he well knows, with much increased effect.

Yet through it all his most reliable instrument, the most mighty and unfailing agent of his power, is just simply words, and again we are brought to the strange magic of those subtle and elusive winged creatures, which have tantalized us and escaped us so many times before. It is words with which the lover tries to bridge his impassable gap, and fails. Words are a tremendous weapon of the dealer in power for social or political purposes. Words are the exquisite material with which the literary artist, the poet, fashions his stuff of immortality. And it is above all words that the preacher uses to penetrate the deepest, darkest corners of men's souls. Words can allure, entice, bewitch, to evil, or to good. Their power of exciting, of stimulating, of damning, of saving, is beyond measure or comparison. And all the time, the preacher is using them in most cases by instinct, with little thought of what their mysterious power is, or as to the nature of its action.

The striking examples of revival fury show perhaps more than anything what this strange force of words may be. These revival manifestations may not be the most dignified or the most enduring effect of words, but they are surely among the most impressive. It is not necessary to dwell upon the extravagant, grotesque features of revivals, the shrieks of distress, the hysterical convulsions, the strange phenomenon called the 'jerks.' It is enough to realize that Edwards, or Finney, or Moody, or Booth, or, if you like, Billy Sunday, could take a vast throng of average men and women, some curious, some indifferent, some contemptuous, and make their spirits quiver and throb and vibrate, like leaves in an autumn wind. The preacher paints the horrors of hell, and men's souls quake with the fear of it. He sets forth the ecstasy of salvation, the splendor of heaven, the glory of God, and men go down on their knees, in agonized entreaty to be made sharers, and partakers, and possessors, of what he has to offer. And all this is accomplished through no other agency whatever but these little, subtle, insignificant, tremendous words.

It is difficult for us to conceive to-day what the power of the pulpit and of the minister through the pulpit was in more believing times. Take early

New England. Not only the moral and religious, but the social, and even the political influence, was largely in ministerial hands. Even up to a hundred years ago the pulpit was the centre from which the intellectual life of the community was mainly disseminated. The minister was the learned man, who was universally looked up to, and who gave light on all topics of interest and importance in every sphere of thought.

Now this is all changed. The churches are too often empty, or when they are filled, it is rather for social than religious purposes. It is perhaps hardly fair to say that the minister is looked down on, where he was once looked up to; but it is certain that the average business man of his congregation regards him with a gentle tolerance, as one whose aims are high, but whose methods and tendencies are rather ludicrously unpractical. The change has come about not only from the general lack of religious belief. It results also from the far greater diffusion of knowledge in the community, by which the minister is no longer considered with awe as the infallible source of all wisdom. And, as I had occasion to point out in discussing the work of Moody, an immense instrument in this diffusion of knowledge, and so in the decay of the pulpit, has been the nineteenth century growth of journalism. The newspaper does what the minister and the Sunday church-going used to do. Men used to get together on Sundays to find out what was going on in the world. Now they can find out more quickly and more satisfactorily by staying at home and reading the Sunday paper. Only the Sunday paper certainly does not perform its mission with an ethical purpose, and the fierce, relentless — and hopeless — war that Moody waged upon the Sunday papers was entirely justified. Whatever their merits, and without in the least aiming at anything of the kind, they are the most dangerous enemies of communal religion.

With the decay of the pulpit and of the clerical influence behind it, has gone an equal decay of the enormous direct priestly influence upon the individual human soul. The most obvious means of exercising this influence was the formal confessional of the Catholic Church, that agency which developed at an early period, grew to have such enormous significance, was indisputably liable to such grave abuses, yet worked such lasting and precious benefit in many directions. For the instinct of confession is one of the most rooted and fundamental impulses of the pervading I, simply one of the forms of the endeavor to get beyond oneself which we have been tracing everywhere. To confide one's troubles, griefs, and sufferings, to confide one's triumphs and hopes, to confide one's life experience of all sorts, this is an unquenchable, an irresistible longing, from which no one is altogether free, and which when it is repressed in one form, is sure to manifest itself in another. Thus, it is interesting to note how in recent days, the influence that used to belong to the minister through this thoroughly human habit, has largely passed to the family physician, and the country doctor has, or had, until the specialist eclipsed him, a surprising store of varied knowledge, not only about the physical ills of his patients, but about their family relations and about all their worldly and even their spiritual affairs in general.

But in the days when men believed that the priest or minister was given the keys of heaven and hell, and the power to bind and to loose, the hold that he had over individual souls is almost incomprehensible to our unbelieving hearts at present. And the richness, the variety, the beauty, the comfort of that hold can hardly be exaggerated. The terrible loneliness that is the greatest curse of life could be largely soothed and mitigated by the quiet touch of one who had soothed so many lives, and penetrated so many secrets. The agony of remorse, the dread of future punishment, the fear of losing the love of God forever, these were real and horrible things once. It is not sure that they have ceased to be horrible, even if the pressure of them is less direct. In any case, the weight of them is immensely diminished, if they can be imparted, and far more, if they can be imparted to one who knows a speedy and efficient cure for them. The records of the direction, the spiritual care and guidance of the great fathers of the Catholic Church, are simply typical of the infinite consolation which the wise and thoughtful priestly comforter has always been able to administer, and no one can look over the vast collection of spiritual letters of Fénelon, or of Saint Francis of Sales, without feeling that the power they exercised was one of the richest and most beneficial that has been given to man. The following long and beautiful passage of Fénelon sums up admirably the various elements involved in such ministry: 'Speak little; listen much; think far more of understanding hearts and of adapting yourself to their needs than of saying clever things to them. Show that you have an open mind, and let every one see by experience that there is safety and consolation in opening his mind to you. Avoid extreme severity, and reprove, where it is necessary, with caution and gentleness. Never say more than is needed, but let whatever you do say be said with entire frankness. Let no one fear to be deceived by trusting you. ... Keep track of all who come to you, and follow them up, if they seem disposed to escape. You should become all things to all the children of God, for the sake of gaining every one of them. And correct yourself, for the sake of correcting others.' [10]

IV

As the curious, watchful search for the persistent I followed us through the effort to overcome it by direct denial, so it follows us in the passionate endeavor to lose the I in the life of others, whether the endeavor is that of the idealists of this world or of those of the next. Penetrating, dispassionate observers have always noted the intrusion of the I in even the most ardent struggles and sacrifices of the reformers and the preachers, and it is not alone the somewhat cynical Montaigne who remarks, 'When I confess myself to myself strictly, I find that the greatest goodness I possess has in it a certain tincture of what is less good.' [11] If you meditate upon what seems at first to be the most unselfish utterance possible, 'I should like the world to be better for my having lived in it,' you see how even here the I is as intrusive and as aggressive as ever.

There are such delightful — or pitiful — indirect forms of this insinuating persistence of the I. For example, there is a type of person whose whole life seems to be given to others, who seeks no pleasure, no amusement, no direct satisfaction for himself, or more often for herself. Yet if you examine closely — too closely — into the motive, you see that all the while the real object is not so much others as the distorted emphasis of the I in the passionate preoccupation with doing one's own duty and satisfying one's own conscience. Sometimes this even takes the extreme form of a deliberate desire to atone for one's real or imagined sins and errors in the past. But more often it is a matter of the haunting torment of conscience, perpetually urging that some duty has been left undone, some obligation neglected, and therefore that one's own life is incomplete and imperfect because one has not filled and rounded it out by the use of others for the purpose for which apparently they were ordained. In these cases you cannot help feeling that the life for others is simply a more emphatic and more intense assertion of life for self. And if this conclusion is resented with regard to many lives which seem to be of the greatest usefulness and value and beauty, the truth of it is best seen when one compares the type of life I refer to, in which the constantly haunting phantom of duty is the unfailing motive, with the life of others who do not bother about duty or conscience in any way whatsoever, who never talk or think about formal religious obligations, yet enter into the lives of those near them with joyous and perfect instinctive sympathy, and perpetually give not because they ought to or are bound to, but from the simple, pure, natural, delightful habit of giving.

So far as this matter of disposing of the I goes, it might be thought that there was at least one form of sacrifice which overcame and got rid of the monster triumphantly and forever. Greater love hath no man than this, that he lay down his life for his friend, unless the principle of love be carried further yet, and he lays down his life for his enemy. In either case, it seems as if there could be nothing left of the I after such a sacrifice. Yet when the analysis is carried a little further, one has one's doubts even here. If it is simply a question of laying down a phenomenal life, if the life in this world is thrown away merely in view of a larger and more glorious life elsewhere, there is obviously no question of overcoming the I at all, merely of developing and enlarging it. Furthermore, in cases where the I is so sacrificed, the circumstances are often such that the life in this world has lost all its value and has become a matter of so much loathing and disgust that the possibility of getting rid of it is delightful in itself, without any question of others in the matter. Also, in the last analysis, we again come across one of those curious and perplexing antinomies and paradoxes of the I. If the social instinct may account for all our sacrifices for others, and if the social instinct is in itself nothing but an indirect form of the instinct of self-preservation, then we have once more simply an instinct going beyond the bounds of its original purpose, and developing unconsciously until it reaches the fantastic result of defeating that purpose altogether.

But we are not obliged to trace the I in these obscure and subtle winding paths, in order to be aware and convinced of its constant intrusion into the work and lives of the idealists in every form. There is simply ambition, the desire to achieve great things, and to be known and honored for having achieved them. Who for a moment questions the presence of such a motive in the altruistic activities of this world? Is not the reformer or the philanthropist often anxious about his reputation and his success and desirous to get the credit of what he has done? He may be quite unaware of this desire and even vehemently repudiate it, which only makes his case more interesting, since the desire is bound to show in his actions, and even in his words at all times. I have happened especially to note the appearance of this ambition in the case of Frances Willard, who was a devoted laborer for the good of others, if ever any one was. Her enthusiastic biographer says of her that her sole aim was 'to do the will of God as far as she knew it.' [12] Yet even into her conscious life there is the undeniable intrusion of a few other little things. She says of herself: 'I have been called ambitious, and so I am, if to have had from childhood the sense of being born to a fate is an element of ambition.' [13] At any rate, there are few more marked symptoms of the aggravated I. And Miss Willard amplifies this confession elsewhere: 'My chief besetments were, as I thought, a speculative mind, a hasty temper, a too ready tongue, and the purpose to be a celebrated person.' [14] The glorious abundance of

I here seems to leave others quite in the background. And Miss Willard is not singular among philanthropists of either sex.

But it will be said that these philanthropists were all people of this world and naturally tainted with this world's weaknesses. Those who live in the spirit and are working to do the will of God move in a higher and unadulterated sphere. It may be so, yet it would seem that even the saints, sometimes by the implication of their words, sometimes by direct confession, are as susceptible to the attractions of glory as their weaker brethren. The strange cry of General Booth, 'I hungered for hell,' [15] that is so that I might get men out of it, would appear to have the same basis as some of the aspirations of Frances Willard. When Saint Francis of Assisi was in prison, he assured his companions that 'some day he would be adored by all the world.' [16] Pascal declared that 'the sweetness of glory is so great that we love it, even if death goes with it.' [17] And a saint of the East sums up the whole matter even more vividly: 'The vanities of all others may die out, but the vanity of a saint as regards his sainthood is hard indeed to wear away.' [18]

Also, besides the ambition which impels, there is the exhilaration, the intoxication, which comes when you are exhorting great masses of people, when you expose to them your plans and efforts and struggles for their good. In an earlier chapter we have seen how great is this excitement of immediate response for the artist, the actor, or musician, who appeals directly to vast audiences and succeeds, or fails, in carrying them away. The excitement is certainly no less when you feel that you are not merely seeking glory for yourself, but are endeavoring to arouse and stimulate your hearers for the benefit of all the world. I know no more naïve, effective statement of this platform intoxication in general than Pepys's record of the success of his great patriotic speech in regard to the navy: 'Everybody do say that the kingdom will ring of my abilities and that I have done myself right for my whole life; and so Captain Cocke, and others of my friends, say that no man had ever such an opportunity of making his abilities known; and, that I may cite all at once, Mr. Lieutenant of the Tower did tell me that Mr. Vaughan did protest to him, and that, in his hearing it, said so to the Duke of Albemarle, and afterwards to W. Coventry, that he had sat twenty-six years in Parliament and never heard such a speech there before; for which the Lord God make me thankful.' [19]

Again, it may be said that the profane, the reformers of this world, may be susceptible to such
human outbursts of vanity, but that those who are
doing the work of God are quite above it. They
often say they are above it, they may even think
they are above it: no doubt they do. Yet there is
abundant evidence to show that the excitement of
public applause and admiration means just as much
to the preacher as to the actor. If people are
touched and moved and stirred by his preaching,
he has succeeded; if they are not, he has failed. And
no man on this earth is perfectly regardless of the
difference between failure and success, or of the
evidences of either. Even preachers of the more
staid and sober type have·the susceptibility in the
keenest form, and the revivalist, who goes from
place to place, perpetually playing upon the passions and emotions of varied audiences, gets to feel
that the excitement of such performance is a necessity of his being. Who does not hear such excitement throbbing through Whitefield's account of
this aspect of his ministry: 'It was wonderful to see
how the people hung upon the rails of the organ
loft, climbed upon the leads of the church, and
made the church itself so hot with their breath that
the steam would fall from the pillars, like drops of

rain. Sometimes almost as many would go away for want of room as came in, and it was with great difficulty I got into the desk to read prayers and preach.' [20]

Also, underlying the immediate excitement, there is the deeper consciousness of power. In a previous chapter we have considered the immense assertion of the I in the acquisition of power over men for selfish purposes. But the power may also be acquired vastly to do men good, and the sense of it and the enjoyment of it may be much the same. The schemer, the dreamer, who evolves ideal utopias, in which all men shall work together for the happiness of all, usually conceives himself as prompter and manager, at least as getting everlasting glory from the design. The practical philanthropist, if he is to succeed, must have the gift of planning, the gift of organizing, the gift of making men work with him and with each other, and the exercise of all these gifts inevitably carries the sense and the joy of power with it. Also, power in the impersonal, the idealistic form, is by no means free from the defects that attend the acquisition and the employment of it for more personal purposes. There is the dogmatism, the immense self-confidence, the almost necessary assurance that you are right and know what should be done and others do not. And with this assurance too often goes an intolerant spirit, the wayward assertion of the I in contempt for others' opinions and for others' methods. Even, as is well known, the most devoted philanthropists are not wholly exempt from the last weakness of the I, its direct pugnacity, and some of the best causes in the world have been fatally injured and disfigured by petty jealousies and quarrels as remote as possible from the spirit of charity and love. The instinct of rebellion and destruction, which we have seen to be too often characteristic of great reform movements, is itself closely identified with the sense of perverted power, and the child, when it is weary of playing with its toys, gets a new and peculiar satisfaction from pulling them to pieces.

Here once more it need not be supposed that the reformers from the point of view of another world are greatly different. Some of the vastest organizers of human effort that have ever lived have been religious teachers, and the exercise of power in the practice of religious, as of other organization, always carries its own delight and satisfaction with it. Among the thousands of wielders of religious power few perhaps have wielded it more widely or more

efficiently than Ignatius Loyola, and Mr. Sedgwick's admirable study of Loyola shows at every
step how the love of power and the use of it were
inherent in his blood: 'The intensely practical
Loyola, who kept his eye on the earth, estimated
human capacities and weaknesses with the nicety
of a diamond-cutter, knew how to play upon hope,
ambition, desire, and fear, was patient, laborious,
contriving, and full of resources.' [21] The description
might as well be applied to Napoleon. A most curious feature, and an enormous augmentation of this
human sense of power, is the feeling in these religious leaders of having God behind them. Over
and over again, always, they protest they are not
doing their own will, that their own will is sunk,
lost, merged, forgotten, in the will of God. Yet, if
you look curiously, you see that there is an inver-
sion here that is easily possible, and usually actual.
Your will is God's will. Yes, but it is just as easy
to find and feel that God's will is your will, and
thus the sense of power is multiplied beyond all
estimation.

And the access to this vast reservoir much mag-
nifies the weaknesses, when they occur, as, alas,
they too frequently do. In these prophets and
preachers the human elements suggested above

show themselves with painful inconsistency. There
is the dogmatism, the obstinacy, the jealousy, the
bickering, the quarrels. My way is the best way,
is God's way, and if the thing cannot be done in my
way, it shall not be done at all. The 'Imitation'
says: 'If God is with us, surely we should be ready
to give up even our own opinions for the sake of
peace.' [22] It is the last, perfect spiritual sacrifice,
and how few reformers, either of this world or of
another, are ready to make it.

Perhaps the broadest, intensest thrill of power
comes in large efforts of organization, in making
masses of men obedient to your will, or to the will
of God acting through you. But the finest, sweetest, most enduring satisfaction comes in power over
individuals, in guiding them, moulding them, helping them, saving them. There are few, there are
none, who do not at some time or other need such
help, and the gift of administering it, with tact,
with patience, with gentleness, and with enduring
effect is one of the most exquisite and one of the
mightiest that a human being can possess. Note
the calm, supreme assurance, with which Saint
Francis of Sales asserts his power in this line, with
the aid of God to support him: 'To a young gentleman who complained to him that nature had given

him no bent whatever for virtue, he said: "Very well; I will admit that you may have as much aversion for virtue as it is possible for any one to have. I assure you, nevertheless, that you can change your nature, and that, provided you will do what I tell you to, you will find no difficulty in being what you ought, and in acquiring the perfection which in your station in life you should possess."'[23] For, as we have seen in our discussion of pure power, nothing in this world gives more the delight of it and of the assertion of the I than to feel that others look up to you and depend upon you.

V

Thus we have the superb procession of the idealists of all sorts and types sweeping onward through the ages. There are some in white or purple robes, with all the insignia of rank and dignity. There are some in humble garments, poor, soiled, ragged, neglected, dwelling in chilly garrets or abandoned corners. There are some who draw multitudes behind them, thrilled and filled by the power of their words. There are some who are perverse, cranky, can only labor alone, yet even alone sometimes do more than all their competitors together. And all of them are trying to make over the world, and the world is in such vast need of making over that even a thousand times as many workers could make little impression upon it. The aims of all this throng are infinitely varied. Some would make men better, some would merely make them happier, some contend that making them better is the only way to make them happy. Some look only at this world, and think that a complete upheaval here would certainly lead to a perfect society, if they could have their way. Some cry out that what happens here is of no moment whatever, and fix their gaze and that of all who heed them only upon what comes or what may come hereafter. And the methods are as diverse as the aims. Some would force men, and some would persuade. Some would insinuate the kingdom of heaven with exquisite gentleness into eager, waiting hearts. Some would thrust it, by violence, if necessary, upon an unwilling and indifferent world. But in all alike there are the qualities of tremendous energy, courage, persistence, confidence, which no difficulty can dishearten, and no failure can overcome.

Yet somehow I feel the deepest sacrifice of the I in quiet lives very different from those of the more flaunted, trumpeted workers. There are men and women, women especially, hidden away in obscure corners all over the world, whose lives are lived for others, from morning till night and from year's end to year's end. In such lives there is no high ideal, there is no subtle, remoter glory. There is just an endless doing of little, tawdry, insignificant, unregarded, hateful things that others may live more comfortably, others who have often no appreciation and no gratitude. Doubtless even in lives like these it would be possible to find the I lurking somewhere, but to seek for it would be an ungracious task. Instead, there seems to be endless, limitless devotion, with no future and no reward. A brief, homely, crude narrative that has come to me lately illustrates the sort of life I mean, with a primitive bareness that makes it all the more impressive, and the character and experience of the narrator are as significant as what he narrates: 'Once a week Irene has an old woman out to the house to do the washin'. Drab-lookin' creature. Pathetic. Long hard-luck story an' all that. Feel kind a' sorry for her each time she gets in front o' my eyes. Well, last week the old dame'd been washin' clothes all day, and I guess was a sight tired. For some reason the maid was out. The old one was waitin' on the table. She looked twice as tired as me. I wasn't fresh myself. For

some reason it kind a' ached me to have her waitin'
on me. When we was through, I went over, took
the old lady by the arm. "Look a' here," I said.
"You come on over an' sit down at this table. I'm
going to wait on you for a change." "Nobody ever
waited on me in my life," she said. "I've waited on
them." "Well," I said, "you're goin' to be waited
on this time." She was kind a' flustered, but I succeeded in gettin' her to sit. Then I went out in the
kitchen an' brought her in a big dish of asparagus.
I cooked some toast an' brought her that, along
with a big cup o' coffee. Then I went into the re-
frigerator an' stole a heapin' saucerful o' straw-
berries an' a big pitcher a' thick cream. Say, you
should 'a' seen that poor old dame eat. And, say,
how she did appreciate it. I felt like I'd done
something worth while in my life, if I never done it
before.' 24

'For whosoever shall give you a cup of water to
drink in my name . . . he shall not lose his reward.' 25
No matter where the I may be in it all, or may
not be, it sometimes seems as if such experiences as
this were the most beautiful thing in our beautiful,
hideous world.

CHAPTER VIII
CHRIST AND I AND GOD

I

THE craving of the I to assert and to escape itself can find no satisfaction in this life. Immediate, direct enjoyment is not enough. Direct denial and subdual are not enough. Even the forgetting of self in others, whether for their good in this world or for their good in another, is not enough. There is always that inevitable, terrible death waiting round the corner, with his whisper, his question, his dread, which some deny, and some drown out, and some forget, but which all feel at one time or another.

And so the I sets itself to the contemplation of its own future in another world, and all it may bring with it. The disagreeable possibilities of hell we have already touched upon. The question of heaven is even more complicated, that is of a mechanical, tangible heaven, a definite place, where the I may develop its vast longings and satisfy its needs in a way quite undreamed of here. The physical location of such a heaven has become a hopeless puzzle. When the universe was more uncertain and unexplored than it is now, the puzzle

was less, and the mediæval sages could map out a
heaven like Dante's with some assurance that the
knowledge of even the vulgar would not too grossly
contradict them. No doubt this mechanical, local
heaven persisted for a long time, and in some minds
still persists. Moody's crude belief brings it vividly
home to me, because I have just been studying
him; but there are still some, perhaps very many,
who cling to views like Moody's and to whom
heaven is a place somewhere above us, with a
definite, if supremely glorious, geography.

There has always been something the same difficulty about the elements of heaven as about its
locality. There are a lot of pleasant things of this
world that we should like to find there, if we spoke
frankly. But so many of the pleasantest things of
this world are directly or indirectly connected with
sin, that it seems inappropriate and indecorous to
associate them with a region where sin is not.
Hence the believer has always fallen back upon the
rather doubtfully agreeable. Crowns and harps and
gates of gold and pavements of pearl, and the unfailing white garb, or no garb at all, may have
certain recommendations, but they do not attract
with any very fierce suggestion of felicity. Even
the continuous concert, which appears to be a last

resort, is not exciting to most types of mind, especially when one considers that the varieties of
music that are most delightful are again apt to be
steeped in the suggestions of sin.

Thus the description of heaven tends to become
lamentably negative, as I have already suggested in
considering the New Testament, and those who
deal with it always have recourse to a bliss which is
mainly composed of the absence of things: no sin,
no sorrow, no hunger, no longing, no separation,
until one is petulantly driven to add, and no anything else. See how curiously and subtly the negative creeps into heaven as depicted by one of the
greatest of the older doctors of the Church: 'And
the life to come is what we have represented to us
by the following character, that it is eternal in
duration, and a blessedness to all eternity, a state
where is the most profound security and tranquil-
lity, pleasure without passion, love without fear,
love in perfection, day without night, activity and
strength without possibility of decay, perfect un-
animity, all the souls in it rapt with the contemplation of God, and past all apprehension of
being ever deprived of his beatific presence.' [1]
Remove the withouts from that passage and there
is something left, but the shrinkage is considerable.

Thus, with the development of astro-physics and the spread of general education, the concrete, material heaven has become lamentably remote and dim. One occasionally meets a simple heart who consoles herself for a somewhat meagre diet here by the proclamation of unlimited cloudy banquets hereafter. But it seems as if the bulk of American men and women gave little thought to a future life in any definite shape. Live here as creditably as you can, do what good you can, and if there is another life, your chance of getting it will be as fair as the next man's. This seems about to sum up the creed of average people, as you meet them every day.

Among the enormous difficulties that the problem of heaven presents take a very prominent one, that of future human connections. It has always been held out as a peculiar claim of heaven that we shall know our friends there. But astonishing complications occur. Will our friends, when we meet them, be different, or will they be the same? If they are to be different, how can they possibly interest us? If they are to be the same, there will be the same old troubles and drawbacks and disappointments that affect our human relations here. We shall still long to dissolve our I in that of others and still be thwarted at every turn. Again, what does it mean

to be the same? Some of those we have loved best
have died years ago, when we and they were young.
Are we to meet them as they were then, or as we are
now? Either would be in the last degree awkward
and unsatisfactory. To take the personal instance.
One of the problems that has always exercised me
most is that of my mother. When she died, I was
three years old, and she was under thirty. I have
naturally no recollection of her, but I have always
cherished her memory as an ideal of many, many
things that life might have given to me and never
has. If I were to meet my mother as she was when
she died, what would she mean to me? I can conceive of her only as one of the young things of her
age, whom I see daily about the streets, perhaps
flippant and tawdry, perhaps sensitive and charming, but in any case so infinitely remote from my
present self that I could address her only with
benevolent patronage or with uncomprehending
awe. No, I think I do not want to meet my mother.
She is the biggest problem of heaven, but she is only
one of them.

II

Yet not the biggest; for the biggest problem is
God. And the mechanical God tends to go much

the same way that the mechanical heaven has gone. Long ago, with the primitive peoples, before astro-physics or any other physics, the natural world was full of gods. The nymphs danced through the woodland with quivering grace, and the stars charioted human deities, who partook of our passions and sometimes shared them, and intervened in human fate, lovingly or angrily, in all its phases. These surprising, enchanting, bewildering, terrifying forms of the supernatural lingered on side by side with Christian conceptions, and it was only by slow degrees that the fairies and the witches faded away into the glimmering ghost of Santa Claus, who now holds the field alone. But through all these wraiths and phantoms of the vanishing supernatural there persisted the dominant, tremendous figure of the mechanical God. To the mass of human beings in the Middle Ages this God was a startlingly intimate, familiar personality, as vivid as a friend, or enemy, waiting to embrace you or assail you round the corner, and in such a form no doubt he persists to-day with simple minds, as he obviously persisted with evangelists of the Moody type and their followers. The mechanical God appears as a benevolent old gentleman, who, being otherwise unoccupied, one day took it into his head to make the universe out of nothing, and has had abundant cause to regret his action ever since. He is figured as much the type of the average human father, good-natured enough when he is well disposed and when he feels that he is treated with proper respect and consideration, but by no means free from senile irascibility, and requiring, like earthly fathers, to be flattered, petted, and caressed; so that his worshippers quickly learn to pattern themselves after the model of the exemplary, favorite child.

The mechanical God is naturally approached with mechanical prayer. If you want a thing, and ask for it long enough and hard enough, you may get it, if it is not too unreasonable, and sometimes even if it is. The attitude of Voltaire's Swiss captain is not altogether exceptional: 'O my God, if there is a God, save my soul, if I have a soul.' [2] But in general it is better to be more earnest about it, and if you have conviction back of you, it goes a long way in getting your prayers answered. In any case, the habit of mechanical prayer, of asking this paternal authority for varied favors, persists with many who have long ceased to have any great confidence that their prayers will be heard.

For it cannot be maintained that God, in the

concrete sense, has the same hold upon mankind that he had a thousand, or a hundred, years ago. From the mechanical point of view men find it hard to take him seriously. While the daily, physical world was full of wonders and surprises, and ordinary phenomena were not at all understood in their general working, it was easy enough to accept and look for divine intervention in common affairs. You could ask a deity to change the course of nature, and as you did not know that there was a course of nature, it seemed easy for him to do it. But when nature became a business of complicated, universally applicable, unalterable laws, the action of God became more and more remote, until the ordinary mind grew indisposed to allow for it at all. And there were the moral difficulties, which became more and more serious, the more men and women became educated and consequently reflective. Here was an omnipotent deity, all-wise, all-good. Yet he had created a world of beings, absolutely dependent upon him, owing him everything, and he had made their lives a simple mass of intolerable misery. It was disconcerting, and all the huge ingenuity of the theologians, in explaining and reconciling, in bullying and intimidating, could not make it any less so.

Hence the mechanical God tended strongly to disappear. The churches emptied, for various reasons, but perhaps chiefly because it did not seem necessary to attend them in order to escape the wrath of a deity who was becoming so very hypothetical. People continued to refer to God with the deepest respect, but the respect was as toward one who after all had very little to do with their daily concerns. It is conveniently alleged that this increased remoteness of the divine is a matter of increasing reverence. It was unseemly, indecorous, to treat God after the mediæval fashion, as if he was a neighbor in the next street, with a rather empty ear yawning to be filled with all the petty gossip of our little human happenings. Reverence is a convenient pretext. But it is somewhat odd that when we have so largely abolished reverence in our own intimate family life, we should make so much of it in the deeper relation, where love should mean far more than even in the home. The disappearance of the mechanical God has come so gradually and is so carefully and skilfully veiled, that we are hardly aware of how thorough and complete it is. In a little poem, written a few years ago, called 'Exit God,' I endeavored to suggest some of the significant phases of this disappearance:

LIFE AND I

Of old our fathers' God was real,
  Something they almost saw,
Which held them to a stern ideal,
  And scourged them into awe.

They walked the narrow path of right
  Most vigilantly well,
Because they feared eternal night
  And boiling depths of hell.

Now hell has wholly boiled away,
  And God become a shade:
There is no place for him to stay
  In all the world he made.

The followers of William James
  Still let the Lord exist,
And call him by imposing names,
  A venerable list.

But nerve and muscle only count,
  Gray matter of the brain,
And an astonishing amount
  Of inconvenient pain.

I sometimes wish that God were back
  In this dark world and wide,
For though some virtues he might lack,
  He had his pleasant side.

III

But the disappearance of the mechanical God does not in the least dispose of the fundamental, essential longing, craving, of the I to get out of itself, somehow, somewhere to achieve a larger, fuller, more complete, enduring existence. Soon, too soon, the I learns that this longing can never be satisfied by any sort of contact with the mere phenomenal creatures around it, or by any love for them. In the magical phrase of the 'Imitation,' 'Qui adhæret creaturæ cadit cum labili.' [3] And still, and always, the yearning I reaches out for some spiritual reality that shall be stable and eternal. It is true that there are plenty of gross, solid, well-poised, thoroughly human natures, who do not make a misery of this longing. Even, that admirable, in the best sense earthly, race of the Greeks seemed to make for itself an ideal in which the longing was quite left out. But more troubled peoples, and certainly those who have been touched by the Christian unearthliness, have the longing in their blood, and the earthly life cannot be satisfying, cannot be perfect, unless it is touched by the unearthly, for which there has been yet found no better word than God. God! What do the three little, mighty letters mean? Who knows? Who cares? Sometimes those who think they know are the ones who care the least. The word means nothing, it means everything, it means the longing of the human soul for a million years, and that is enough. 'She was one of those souls who are hungry for eternity,' says the French critic.⁴ But we are all hungry for eternity; only some of us drown the hunger, or forget it, as best we can. 'Thou hast made us to incline to thee,' said Augustine, 'and our hearts are restless and tormented, until in thee they find their peace.'⁵

There is the approach to God through nature, through the varied allurement and charm of the external world. And this approach is facilitated by the habit of solitude, which the love of nature so greatly tends to encourage. Alone in vast sweeps of windless woodland or by the unceasing flow of waters, in the silence broken only by the murmurs of nature, the I is stilled in its petulant intrusion, or even more, dissolved in immensity and permanence. As Obermann expresses it, though haunted as always by his sceptical questioning: 'If I arrive at old age, if, one day, full of thoughts still, but no longer conversing with mankind, I have near me a friend to receive my last farewell to earth, let him place my chair upon the shorn turf, and let there be a field of tranquil daisies, under the sunlight, under the immensity of heaven, so that, as I leave this life which flits away, I may regain something of the Illusion that is infinite.' [6] And Shelley renders the experience with even more vivid ardor:

> That light whose smile kindles the universe,
>   That beauty in which all things work and move,
> That benediction which the eclipsing curse
>   Of birth can quench not, that sustaining love,
>   Which through the web of being blindly wove
> By man and beast and earth and air and sea,
>   Burns bright or dim as each are mirrors of
> The fire for which all thirst, now beams on me,
> Consuming the last clouds of cold mortality.[7]

Or, without the intermediation of nature, there is the direct communion of the mystic with the inner fire and the inner light, the supersensual vision grasping intuitively that vast final something, which those who are not vouchsafed the vision or the intuition can but dimly understand.

There is the strange mysticism of the East, coming to most of us only through the broken, troubled medium of a pedantic, distorted language which cannot fail to hamper and betray. Yet even through that medium there are glimpses of the rapturous deliverance, the boundless peace, which are given to the sage who can still the turmoil of passion and sway the mighty, turbulent, rebellious I whither he will. The supreme abandonment, the final identification with the divine unity, no doubt has its difficulties for us who are unenlightened, and it somehow seems to us that the element of negation still clings to it unduly. But the charm is there, the enthralling allurement, the suggestion of a peace which this world cannot give: 'In the beginning Brahman was all this. He was one, and infinite; infinite in the East, infinite in the South, infinite in the West, infinite in the North, above and below and everywhere infinite. East and the other regions do not exist for him, nor across, nor below, nor above. The Highest Self is not to be fixed, he is unlimited, unborn, not to be reasoned about, not to be conceived. He is like the ether (everywhere), and at the destruction of the universe he alone is awake. Thus from that ether he wakes all this world, which consists of thought only, and by him is all this meditated on, and in him it is dissolved. ... He who knows this becomes one with the One.' [8] Or as our own Emerson, who felt the charm so profoundly, renders it: 'The soul is not born; it does not die; it was not produced from any one. Nor was any produced from it. ... Thinking the soul as unbodily among bodies, firm among fleeting things, the wise man casts off all grief. The soul cannot be gained by knowledge, not by understanding, not by manifold science. It can be obtained by the soul by which it is desired. It reveals its own truths.' 9

And there is the mysticism of Christianity, which uses our own terms, our own symbols, with which we have grown up from childhood, and which has come to us not in a distorted pedantic medium, but through the grandest, subtlest forms of imaginative and intellectual ardor. No doubt the simpler spiritual insight has been seized upon by the theologians and worked over with their strange processes of intellectualization till it sometimes seems as if the ardor had gone out of it and given place to the chill obscurity of thought. Augustine is not content with emotional receptiveness, but strives to penetrate and inform it with his subtle metaphysical question: 'Thou art not dissipated, but Thou gatherest us. But Thou who fillest all things fillest Thou them with Thy whole self? Or, since all things cannot contain Thee wholly, do they contain part of Thee? And all at once the same part? Or each its own part, the greater more, the smaller less? And is, then, one part of Thee greater, another less? Or art Thou wholly everywhere, while nothing contains Thee wholly?' [10] Aquinas seeks to make theoretical propositions out of what would seem to be more fitly spiritual experience: 'It remains that man's final felicity consists in the contemplation of wisdom pursuant to a consideration of things divine. From which it also is evident by the way of induction what was before proved by arguments, that the final felicity of man consists only in the contemplation of God.' [11]

And the more professed metaphysicians subject the divine experience still more to the elaborate methods of logical treatment. Spinoza develops the identity of the universe with Deity by a process of reasoning similar to the deductions of pure mathematics. And again, after Kant's remorseless analysis has swept away such logical devices, the German philosophers patiently rebuild the metaphysical edifice of deity, each in his own elaborate Teutonic fashion. And through it all one is reminded of the profound saying of Goethe in regard to one of the greatest of such metaphysical mystics: 'Everything Spinozistic in poetry becomes in speculative thinking Machiavelism.' [12] Yet even as to this same Spinoza, when his enemies charged him with being an atheist, his admirers could cry out that he was 'a man intoxicated with God.'

As a side issue, or minor development, of this intellectual mysticism, we have the complicated symbolism of the German Boehme or of Swedenborg, in which an inspired interpreter seeks and reveals with supreme self-assurance the subtle correspondences between the world of material things and the world of the spirit. It will always remain an intellectual curiosity, perhaps singularly revealing for the temper of Emerson himself, that he should have chosen Swedenborg as the mystical type; since, in spite of ampler and more human sides of his teaching and of undeniable power of spiritual insight, he gives the sense, far more than do even Augustine and Aquinas, of unbridled ratiocination let loose to work its disastrous way among the delicate and evanescent raptures of the mystical ecstasy.

IV

For the centre, the kernel of Christian mystical experience is feeling, emotion, love, to use the word which is so well worn and so liable to misinterpretation, but to which the great mystics infallibly have recourse, love of something which is the object of the unappeasable longing, or the desire that cannot be stilled. It may be the love of Christ, as typifying, personifying, embodying the divine, 'all things are loved for the sake of Jesus, but Jesus for himself,' as the 'Imitation' has it; [13] or it may be the love of God direct. The feeling may be guided, governed, inspired, by reasoned belief; but without the feeling, the belief is dull, dry, barren, and ineffectual.

And here, in this central aspect of the spiritual life, we find prayer again, as a very different instrument from the mere mechanical device by which a persistent child solicits a weary parent for practical advantages and benefits. Prayer here becomes a means of communion, of escaping from common needs and superficial distractions, and of burying oneself in the infinite, inexhaustible depths of the divine. It may be a matter of prayer in actual words. It may be simply the loss of the immediate present and trivial external surroundings in the rapture of absorbed contemplation; but always the end, the aim, is the surrender of one's own narrow, personal will to the larger will by which the universe moves and has its being. As Saint Teresa puts it, of the action of prayer: 'Those who are able thus to enclose themselves within the little heaven of their souls where dwells the Creator of

both heaven and earth, and who can accustom themselves not to look at anything nor to remain in any
place which would preoccupy their exterior senses,
may feel sure that they are traveling by an excellent way, and that they will certainly attain to
drink of the water from the fountain, for they will
journey far in a short time." [14]

Naturally psychological analysts in all ages, and
particularly the enthusiastic followers of the 'new
psychology' have busied themselves with the morbid elements of this mystical absorption. No doubt
there are plenty of morbid and fantastic elements
there, and weak minds have sometimes been led
astray and irreparably unhinged by them. There are
the trances and the hallucinations and the visions.
There are the extravagant experiences, like that
of the saint of the mediæval Italian revival: 'She
could not hear God, or Our Lady, or Saint Francis,
mentioned, without at once going into an ecstasy,
"and in this state being filled with superhuman emotions, she knew nothing whatever of what went on
about her. . . . At times she was suspended in the
air, without touching anything, without resting her
feet upon the earth, except the tips of her great
toes. . . . The first time King Charles saw her in
this condition, he wished to try whether her rapture

was real. . . . He had melted lead prepared in quantity, and ordered it to be poured boiling over her naked feet, in his presence. The saint did not feel it in the least."' [15] Discounting the miraculous, one finds the hysterical element in such performances obvious enough. The psychologist is disposed to connect it with all sorts of physiological conditions, and the newly revealed action of mysterious glands may be called upon to explain saintly rapture as well as a great many other things. Above all, the devotee of sex theories finds an ample and luxuriant field in the experiences of the mystics. A glowing language of love, closely approaching that of sexual passion, is so usual in them that the approximation is almost inevitable, and many features undoubtedly suggest the sexual aspect of the matter. The truth is, however, that it is not, or not largely, a question of the physical elements of sex, but that at the bottom of both sexual love and of divine love there lies that fundamental spiritual longing which we have emphasized in our first chapter. In both there is the boundless, illimitable desire of the I to escape, to enlarge itself, to identify its poor, weak, limited, and inadequate existence, with some larger life, which it surmises, aspires to, but cannot attain.

And from this point of view there is something noble, something ideal, something ineffably rich and magnificent, even to one who can only divine it from afar, in the raptures of this mystical communion and spiritual abandonment. And note that it is by no means confined to hysterical, emotional natures, in whom feeling altogether outbalances intellectual power. The greatest of the saints had oftentimes practical ability and common sense, of a high order, had the power of dealing with earthly affairs with the most adequate comprehension and swift efficiency. It is on the testimony of such men and women as these that we must take the spiritual rapture for what it is worth and recognize, even when it seems beyond our grasp, something high and rare which can hardly be surpassed or matched in any other phase of human experience. The expression of the cool, sceptical, critical Erasmus, 'The ecstasy of the saints is no more than a foretaste of the future bliss with which we shall all be absorbed in God, in that future becoming God and ceasing to be ourselves,' [16] is merely the text on which the more elaborate analyses of the saints are so richly embroidered. Saint John of the Cross sums it up with intense, vivid brevity: 'And thus, when the soul has cast off from itself everything that controverts and does not conform to the will of God, it becomes transformed into God by the office of love.' [17]

Naturally it is not to be supposed that even the saints have access to these raptures at all times, or can sustain the highest pitch of them unbroken. The ardor of spiritual exaltation, like other more earthly excitements, brings its reactions with it, and the height of ecstasy is too often succeeded by corresponding depths of discouragement, depression, aridity, and barrenness. These almost inexplicable variations of spiritual response are admirably indicated by Saint Teresa: 'Again, I feel such courage that there is nothing I should fear to do in God's service, and I find, when it comes to the proof, that I am brave sometimes — yet, next day, I should not venture to kill an ant for Him if I met with any opposition. Sometimes I care nothing if people talk or complain of me; and indeed very often it has even given me pleasure. Yet there are occasions when a single word disturbs me and I long to leave this world, for everything in it disgusts me.' [18] Fenelon illustrates the same complications with an almost despairing depth of analysis: 'It seems to me that I love God to madness when I make no endeavor to do so. If I seek the love, I find it no longer. What seems to me true as I first think it, becomes a lie on my lips when I try to utter it. My heart finds no relief, yet if you ask me how I suffer, I find it impossible to explain it to you. . . . From one point of view, the merest trifles amuse me; yet my heart remains dry and utterly dead. And even as I write these words, I seem to myself to be lying, and all my thought is confusion.' [19] And the 'Imitation' has the final word on this, as on other states: 'Thou canst not always continue in a more than usually fervent desire of goodness, nor stand in a degree of contemplation higher than thy wont; but it must needs be that thou shouldest from time to time descend to lower things by reason of original corruption, and shouldest even unwillingly and wearily bear the burden of this corruptible life (et onus corruptibilis vitæ, etiam invite, et cum tædio, portare).' [20]

Then the splendor returns, and the presence of God descends once more, sometimes slowly, like a creeping tide, sometimes in an overwhelming outburst of sudden glory. Of all the expressions of mystical rapture in the variety of saints that I have studied I have found none more rare and more richly suggestive than that given by our own Jonathan Edwards, and said to render the experience of his wife. I have quoted this elsewhere in connection with Moody, but it cannot be quoted too often: 'The soul remained in a kind of heavenly elysium and did, as it were, swim in the rays of Christ's love, like a little mote swimming in the beams of the sun that come in at a window. The heart was swallowed up in a kind of glow of Christ's love coming down as a constant stream of sweet light, at the same time the soul all flowing out in love to him; so that there seemed to be a constant flowing and reflowing from heart to heart. The soul dwelt on high, was lost in God, and seemed almost to leave the body. The mind dwelt in a pure delight that fed and satisfied it, enjoying pleasure without the least sting or any interruption. . . . What was enjoyed in a single minute of the whole space, which was many hours, was worth more than the outward comfort and pleasure of the whole life put together.' [21] If the world has possibilities of such ecstasy as that, surely it is worth our while to know something about them.

Then the cold, critical, insistent analysis of the intellect intervenes. The basis, the central point of all this eternal longing and craving of the I would seem to be the endless conflict between multiplicity and unity. The I is the triumph, the climax, the incarnation of multiplicity. It can find its peace only in complete identity, in absorption in the One, in the Unity which is all pervading and final. Yet, as Pascal says, 'Unity and multiplicity, . . . it is an error to exclude either of the two.' Multiplicity is distinction, variety, life. Absolute unity is peace, repose, and also how is it in any way distinguishable from death? As I find the matter stated in a startling little poem from the Italian of Lulli, called 'The Cross of Naught':

> There exists
> an implacable cross,
> which is *Naught*.
> *All* is nailed
> to this cross.

The I is perpetually torn between two desires. It longs to keep its identity and to lose it, to be forever merged in Nirvana, yet somehow to retain the delicious sense that it is merged, that is, still, still, not to be merged at all.

So far speaks the intellect. But there is always the heart. As LaBruyère has it: 'Shall I dare to say that it is the heart alone that has power to reconcile extremes and to bring together things that seem forever incompatible?' And as regards the intellect, the I has the blessed boon of inconceivable ignorance, which leaves the heart its way. Thus, to the end — and what is the end? — the I continues to assert, to worship, to glorify, and to abominate itself, and after all its infinitely weary struggles, and efforts, and despairs, it asks but one thing, illimitable hope, which no power in the universe can altogether deny it.

THE END

NOTES

I: LOVE AND I

1. First sentence of essay on 'History.'
2. Quoted in an editorial in the Boston *Transcript*, September 18, 1926.
3. *Memoirs, Journal, and Correspondence of Thomas Moore*, vol. III, p. 367, August 29, 1822.
4. Darwin to Asa Gray, July 23, 1862, *More Letters of Charles Darwin*, vol. I, p. 202.
5. Compton Mackenzie, *Old Men of the Sea*, p. 284.
6. Meilhac and Halévy, *La Belle Hélène*, act I, scene 6.
7. *Idyl* VIII.
8. Jane Austen to Cassandra Austen, September 5, 1796.
9. Quoted as epigraph of the second canto of Musset's *Namouna*.
10. Sonnet, *To A Friend*.
11. Jowett's translation of Plato, American edition, vol. II, p. 149.
12. *Imaginary Conversations* (edition Dent), *Conversation between Tibullus and Messala*, vol. II, p. 86.
13. *Les Caractères*, chapter, *Du Cœur*.
14. William McDougall, *Outline of Abnormal Psychology*, p. 331.
15. *Memoirs, Journal, and Correspondence of Thomas Moore*, vol. IV, p. 199, May 22, 1824.
16. Carmina, LXXXV (edition Mueller).
17. Epigraph to *Das Buch Le Grand*.
18. Jones Very, Sonnet, *Beauty, Poems* (1883), p. 154.
19. Mrs. Blaine to Manley, June 4, 1876, *Letters of Mrs. James G. Blaine*, vol. I, p. 136.
20. Poem *To Marguerite*, in the series *Switzerland*.

II: POWER AND I

1. Quoted in Sainte-Beuve, *Nouveaux Lundis*, vol. V, p. 424.
2. *Essais*, book III, chapter IX, *De la Vanité* (édition Louandre, vol. IV, p. 110).

3. *Diary* (edition Wheatley), March 2, 1669, vol. VIII, p. 227.
4. Boswell's *Johnson* (American edition, 1807), vol. II, p. 153.
5. Gray to Wharton, Dec. 11, 1746, *Letters* (edition Tovey), vol. I, p. 150.
6. William Lincoln Palmer, in *Zion's Herald*, Sept. 29, 1926.
7. To Argental, June 21, 1761, *Correspondance de Voltaire* (édition Garnier, 1881), vol. IX, p. 330.
8. Mademoiselle de l'Espinasse, quoted in Sainte-Beuve, *Causeries du Lundi*, vol. II, p. 100.
9. *Maximen und Reflexionen*, dritte Abtheilung.
10. Cromwell to Crawford, March 10, 1643, Carlyle's *Cromwell*, vol. I, p. 171.
11. Cromwell to Fleetwood, 1652, Carlyle's *Cromwell*, vol. II, p. 259.
12. Chesterfield to his son, July 25, 1741.
13. In M. L. Avary, *Dixie after the War*, p. 71.
14. Cardinal de Retz, quoted in Sainte-Beuve, *Port-Royal*, vol. I, p. 487.
15. Madame de Sévigné to Madame de Grignan, July 12, 1671, *Lettres de Madame de Sévigné* (smaller edition), vol. I, p. 354.
16. Madame de Rémusat, *Mémoires*, vol. I, p. 242.
17. J. William Jones, *Life and Letters of Robert Edward Lee*, p. 208.
18. Cromwell to Wraye, July 30, 1643, Carlyle's *Cromwell*, vol. III, p. 235.
19. To Roederer (verbal), quoted in Sainte-Beuve, *Causeries du Lundi*, vol. VIII, p. 292.
20. *Ibid.*, p. 306.
21. *Battles and Leaders of the Civil War*, vol. II, p. 551.
22. Quoted in Sainte-Beuve, *Causeries du Lundi*, vol. IX, p. 26.
23. Saint-Simon, *Mémoires* (édition Hachette, 1884), vol. V, p. 194.
24. Quoted in Sainte-Beuve, *Causeries du Lundi*, vol. VII, p. 382.
25. Quoted in Philip Guedalla, *Fathers of the Revolution*, p. 258.
26. In Carlyle's *Cromwell*, vol. III, p. 192.
27. Napoleon to Vice-President of the Senate, *Correspondance de Napoléon*, vol. IX, p. 251.
28. Quoted in Gaston Boissier, *Cicéron et Ses Amis*, p. 173.

NOTES

III: BEAUTY AND I

1. Eugénie de Guérin, *Journal*, May 22, 1839, p. 273.
2. Nathaniel Field, *A Woman is a Weathercock*, act III, scene 2.
3. *Journal des Goncourt*, March 3, 1862, vol. II, p. 12.
4. *Ibid.*
5. Sonnet XXVI.
6. Sonnet, *The Human Seasons*.
7. Flaubert to Bouilhet, May 24, 1855, *Correspondance*, vol. III, p. 14.
8. Cowper to Newton, May 3, 1780, *Correspondence*, vol. I, p. 185.
9. Keats to Bailey, March 13, 1818, *Letters* (Colvin), p. 43.
10. Keats to Reynolds, August 25, 1819, *Letters*, p. 282.
11. Flaubert to George Sand, Oct. 28, 1872, *Correspondance entre Flaubert et George Sand*, p. 338.
12. *Journal*, March 3, 1852, vol. I, p. 37.
13. Cowper to Lady Hesketh, May 15, 1786, *Correspondence*, vol. III, p. 36.
14. *Pericles and Aspasia*, Letter L.
15. Cowper to Newton, April 22, 1785, *Correspondence*, vol. II, p. 314.
16. Flaubert to Madame X, 1853, *Correspondance de Flaubert*, vol. II, p. 359.
17. Keats to Haydon, May 11, 1817, *Letters*, p. 15.
18. Cowper to Lady Hesketh, April 3, 1786, *Correspondence*, vol. III, p. 7.
19. Voltaire to D'Argental, July 22, 1764, *Correspondance* (édition Garnier, 1881), vol. V, p. 450.
20. Flaubert to Madame X, 1853, *Correspondance*, vol. II, p. 343.
21. Flaubert to Madame X, 1853, *Correspondance*, vol. II, p. 238.
22. Meilhac and Halévy, *La Cigale*, act III, scene 3.
23. Gray to Wharton, June 18, 1858, *Letters* (edition Tovey), vol. II, p. 31.
24. Voltaire to Helvétius, February 25, 1739, *Correspondance* (édition Garnier), vol. III, p. 187.
25. Cowper to Newton, September 18, 1781, *Correspondence*, vol. I, p. 356.
26. Flaubert to Madame X, 1853, *Correspondance*, vol. II, p. 231.

NOTES

27. George Sand to Maurice Sand, March 1, 1864, *Correspondance*, vol. v, p. 16.
28. Voltaire to Fyot de la Marche, October 20, 1761, *Correspondance*, vol. ix, p. 483.

IV: THOUGHT AND I

1. Voltaire to Helvétius, October 27, 1760, *Correspondance* (édition Garnier), vol. ix, p. 40.
2. Quoted in *Life of Darwin*, by Francis Darwin, vol. ii, p. 350.
3. Voltaire to Tressan, November 12, 1760, *Correspondance*, vol. ix, p. 61.
4. Darwin to Hooker, Dec. 11, 1860, *Life of Darwin*, vol. ii, p. 148.
5. Darwin to Lyell, June 1, 1867, *Life of Darwin*, vol. ii, p. 248.
6. Darwin to Scott, July 2, 1863, *More Letters of Charles Darwin*, vol. ii, p. 323.
7. *Pensées, De la Conversation*, xlv.
8. Darwin to Hooker, July 28, 1868, *More Letters of Charles Darwin*, vol. i, p. 305.
9. Darwin to Wiesner, October 25, 1881, *Life of Darwin*, vol. ii, p. 510.
10. *Essais* (édition Louandre), book iii, chapter viii, *L'Art de Conférer*, vol. iv, p. 12.
11. Darwin to Henslow, April 1, 1848, *More Letters of Charles Darwin*, vol. i, p. 61.
12. Vauvenargues to Mirabeau, quoted in Sainte-Beuve, *Causeries du Lundi*, vol. xiv, p. 30.
13. *Maximen und Reflexionen*, zweite Abtheilung.
14. Landor, *Imaginary Conversations* (edition Dent), vol. iii, p. 176, *Lord Brooke and Sir Philip Sidney*.
15. *Maximen und Reflexionen*, dritte Abtheilung.
16. Sainte-Beuve, *Portraits Littéraires*, vol. iii, p. 468.
17. Voltaire to Frédéric Guillaume, Nov. 24, 1770, *Correspondance* (édition Garnier), vol. xv, p. 265.
18. *Pensées, De la Conversation*, lix.
19. *Maximen und Reflexionen*, erste Abtheilung.
20. William McDougall, *Outline of Abnormal Psychology*, p. 480.

NOTES

21. *Essais* (édition Louandre), *De l'Expérience*, book III, chapter XIII, vol. IV, p. 261.
22. Amiel, *Journal*, Dec. 23, 1866, vol. I, p. 234.
23. Voltaire to the Duc d'Uzès, Sept. 18, 1750, *Correspondance* (édition Garnier), vol. V, p. 175.
24. To Manning, January 2, 1810, *Letters* (edition Ainger), vol. I, p. 257.
25. *Essais* (édition Louandre), *De la Physionomie*, book III, chapter XII, vol. IV, p. 205.
26. Jefferson to Isaac Story, Dec. 5, 1801, Jefferson's *Works* (Memorial edition), vol. X, p. 299.
27. *Essais, De l'Expérience*, book III, chapter XIII, vol. IV, p. 262.
28. *Vie de Jésus* (1899), p. xxi.

V: CHRIST AND I

1. Sainte-Beuve, *Causeries du Lundi*, vol. XIII, p. 171.
2. *First Thessalonians*, V, 21.
3. *Vie de Jésus* (édition 1899), p. xcii.
4. *Matthew*, XXVI, 42.
5. *Port-Royal*, vol. III, p. 177.
6. *Mark*, XII, 17.
7. *John*, VIII, 7.
8. *Luke*, VII, 35.
9. *Luke*, XVI, 8.
10. *John*, XIV, 27.
11. *Matthew*, XI, 28.
12. *Matthew*, XII, 48.
13. *Luke*, XVIII, 2.
14. *Luke*, XII, 29.
15. *Luke*, VI, 27.
16. *Luke*, XVII, 21.
17. *Matthew*, XVIII, 3.
18. *First John*, IV, 8, 10.
19. *John*, VIII, 58.
20. *John*, XI, 25.
21. *John*, X, 30.
22. *Matthew*, XI, 27.

NOTES

23. *Matthew*, XXVII, 46.
24. *John*, III, 16.
25. *Matthew*, XXI, 43.
26. Oswald Spengler, *The Decline of the West* (trans. Atkinson), p. 360.
27. *Les Apôtres* (1899), p. 212.
28. Darwin to Wallace, August, 1872, *Life of Darwin*, vol. II, p. 347.
29. Frederick to Voltaire, February 10, 1767, *Correspondance de Voltaire* (édition Garnier), vol. XIII, p. 104.
30. *John*, II, 15.
31. *Les Apôtres* (1899), p. 377.
32. *Philippians*, II, 21.
33. *Imitation*, book I, chap. XIV.
34. *Matthew*, X, 39.

VI: CHRIST AND NOT–I

1. Madame Du Deffand to Walpole, Nov. 20, 1771, *Lettres de Madame Du Deffand à Horace Walpole*, vol. II, p. 311.
2. Quoted by James H. Leuba, in article in *Journal of American Psychology*, April, 1896, vol. VII, p. 324.
3. Pascal, *Pensées*, XXIV, 35.
4. *Sinners in the Hands of an Angry God*, in *Works* (London, 1835), vol. II, p. 9.
5. Hitchcock, *Life of Mary Lyon*, p. 155.
6. Voltaire to Des Hauterais, Dec. 21, 1760, *Correspondance* (édition Garnier), vol. IX, p. 105.
7. Voltaire to Florain, April 7, 1770, *Correspondance*, vol. XV, p. 43.
8. Letter of Deleyre, quoted in Sainte-Beuve, *Nouveaux Lundis*, vol. IV, p. 349.
9. Charles G. Finney, *Memoirs*, p. 263.
10. Alfred C. Underwood, *Conversion, Christian and Non-Christian*, p. 158.
11. Quoted in James, *Varieties of Religious Experience*, p. 209.
12. Quoted in James, *Varieties of Religious Experience*, p. 248.
13. Quoted by George Adam Smith, in *Outlook*, Jan. 20, 1900, vol. LXIV, p. 164.
14. Underwood, *Conversion*, p. 223.

NOTES

15. Madame de Sévigné to Madame de Grignan, June 21, 1680, *Lettres* (small edition), vol. v, p. 78.
16. *Imaginary Conversations* (edition Dent), vol. iv, p. 51, *Rousseau and Malesherbes.*
17. *Pensées,* xxiv, 60.
18. John B. Gough, *Autobiography and Personal Recollections,* p. 86.
19. *Pensées, De l'Education,* xxix.
20. *Journal,* Feb. 17, 1838, p. 159.
21. Pepys, *Diary,* Nov. 19, 1668, vol. viii, p. 149.
22. Tyerman, *Life of John Wesley,* vol. i, p. 436.
23. Quoted in Jules Lemaître, *Fénelon,* p. 262.
24. *Imitation,* book i, chapter vii.
25. *Essais* (édition Louandre), book ii, chapter xvii, *De la Présomption,* vol. iii, p. 89.
26. James, *Varieties of Religious Experience,* p. 311.
27. Saint Teresa, *The Way of Perfection* (translation by the Benedictines of Stanbrook), p. 61.
28. Emile Gebhart, *L'Italie Mystique,* p. 227.
29. *Imitation,* book i, chapter xx.
30. *Imitation,* book ii, chapter ii.
31. Orville Dewey, *Letters of an English Traveler to his Friend in England on the Revivals of Religion,* p. 64.
32. Quoted in Jules Lemaître, *En Marge des Vieux Livres,* vol. ii, p. 262.
33. In Saint-Beuve, *Causeries du Lundi,* p. 13.
34. Henry Dwight Sedgwick, *Ignatius Loyola,* p. 336.

VII: CHRIST AND MORE THAN I

1. *The Fo-Sho-Hing-Tsan-King* (translation Beal), i, 5, p. 48.
2. Renan, *Les Apôtres* (1899), p. 302.
3. Keats to Bailey, Nov. 1, 1817, *Lettres* (edition Colvin), p. 38.
4. Sainte-Beuve, *Causeries du Lundi,* vol. x, p. 298.
5. Meilhac and Halévy, *Barbe-Bleue,* act iii, scene 2.
6. *Essais* (édition Louandre), book iii, chapter ix, *De la Vanité,* vol. iv, p. 80.
7. *Mark,* ii, 17.
8. *Fo-Sho-Hing-Tsan-King* (trans. Beal), i, 2.

NOTES

9. Henry Dwight Sedgwick, *Ignatius Loyola*, p. 43.
10. Fénelon to his niece, July 19, 1712, *Lettres Spirituelles*, xxiv.
11. *Essais* (édition Louandre), book ii, chapter xx, *Nous de Goûtons Rien de Pur*, vol. iii, p. 117.
12. Frances Willard, *Glimpses of Fifty Years*, Introduction, p. v.
13. *Glimpses of Fifty Years*, p. 687.
14. *Glimpses of Fifty Years*, p. 625.
15. Quoted in *Outlook*, Sept. 26, 1908, vol. xc, p. 175.
16. Quoted in Henry Osborn Taylor, *The Medieval Mind*, vol. i, p. 437.
17. *Pensées*, iii, 2.
18. Ramakrishna, in James, *Varieties of Religious Experience*, p. 365.
19. Pepys, *Diary*, March 16, 1668, vol. vii, p. 329.
20. William C. Conant, *Narratives of Remarkable Conversions and Revival Incidents*, p. 24.
21. Henry Dwight Sedgwick, *Ignatius Loyola*, p. 44.
22. *Imitation*, book i, chapter ix.
23. *Œuvres* (édition 1833), vol. xii, p. 271.
24. Communicated to me by Mr. Arthur Crew Inman.
25. *Mark*, ix, 41.

VIII: CHRIST AND I AND GOD

1. Saint Augustine, *Meditations*, book ii, chapter xviii.
2. Voltaire to Madame Du Deffand, May 25, 1770, *Correspondance de Voltaire* (édition Garnier), vol. xv, p. 87.
3. *Imitation*, book ii, chapter vii.
4. Sainte-Beuve, *Port-Royal*, vol. ii, p. 312.
5. Saint Augustine, *Confessions*, book i, chapter i.
6. Sénancour, *Obermann*, p. 425.
7. Shelley, *Adonais*, stanza liv.
8. *Maitrâyana-Brâhmana Upanishad* (translation Müller), vi, 17.
9. Emerson, *Letters and Social Aims* (Riverside edition), p. 333.
10. Saint Augustine, *Confessions*, book i, chapter iii.
11. Quoted in Henry Osborn Taylor, *The Mediæval Mind*, vol. ii, p. 476.
12. Goethe, *Maximen und Reflexionen*, dritte Abtheilung.
13. *Imitation*, book ii, chapter viii.

NOTES

14. Saint Teresa, *The Way of Perfection* (translated by the Benedictines of Stanbrook), p. 161.
15. Emile Gebhart, *L'Italie Mystique*, p. 207.
16. Erasmus to Dorp, 1515, *Erasmi Epistolæ* (edition Allen), vol. ii, p. 103.
17. San Juan de la Cruz, *Obras* (edition Biblioteca de Autores Españoles, vol. i), p. 23, *Subida de Monte Carmelo*, book i, chapter v.
18. Saint Teresa, *The Way of Perfection*, p. 235.
19. Quoted in Jules Lemaître, *Fénelon*, p. 325.
20. *Imitation*, book iii, chapter li.
21. Jonathan Edwards, *Thoughts on the Revival*, part i, section v, Works (London, 1835), vol. i, p. 376.
22. *Pensées*, xxiv, 70.